EMANUEL

INDEX VOLUME

SUPPLEMENTS

TO

VETUS TESTAMENTUM

EDITED BY
THE BOARD OF THE QUARTERLY

VOLUME XCIV,2

EMANUEL

STUDIES IN HEBREW BIBLE
SEPTUAGINT
AND DEAD SEA SCROLLS

IN HONOR OF
EMANUEL TOV

INDEX VOLUME

BRILL
LEIDEN · BOSTON
2003

This book is printed on acid-free paper.

Photo credit: the frontispiece photograph in the text volume was made by David Harris, Yemin Moshe, Jerusalem.

BS
1171.3
.E43
2003
Suppl.

Bibliographic information published by Die Deutsche Bibliothek

Die Deutsche Bibliothek lists this publication in the Deutsche Nationalbibliographie; detailed bibliographic data are available on the Internet at http://dnb.dde.de.

Library of Congress Cataloging-in-Publication Data

Library of Congress Cataloging-in-Publication Data is also available.

ISSN 0083-5889
ISBN 90 04 13006 3 (*index volume*)
ISBN 90 04 12679 1 (*text volume*)
ISBN 90 04 13007 1 (*set*)

CONTENTS

INDEX OF ANCIENT SOURCES

(A) Hebrew Bible/Old Testament

Genesis (Gen)

1:1–5	551
1:2	525 n. 2, 536 n. 37
1:14	96
1:27	298
1:31	835
2	523 n. 20
2:2	217
2:5	847
2:6	536 n. 37
2:7	537, 847
2:12	536 n. 37
2:14	536 n. 37
2:17	536 n. 37
2:20	536 n. 37
3:1	536 n. 37
3:3	536 n. 37
3:8	66
3:11	518
3:14	529 n. 16
3:15	619 n. 3
3:17	536 n. 37
3:21	843 n. 34
4:1	525 n. 2, 536 n. 37
4:2	525 n. 2, 536 n. 37
4:3–4	537
4:5	525 n. 2, 536 n. 37
4:7	536 n. 37
4:8	287
4:9a	536 n. 38
4:9b	525 n. 2
4:10	536 n. 38
4:13	536 n. 38
4:15	536 n. 38
4:16	525 n. 2, 536 n. 38
4:18	537
4:22	537
4:23	537
4:25	525 n. 2, 537
6:2	538
6:4	538 n. 41
6:5	340
6:5–6	538
6:7–12	163
6:8	538 n. 41
6:9	538 n. 41
6:10	538
6:11	538
6:13	756 n. 11
7:7	538
7:9	298
7:10	538
7:12	538 n. 43
7:17	538 n. 43
8:6	538 n. 43
8:13	538 n. 43
9:4	675 n. 2
9:6	847
9:24	536 n. 38
9:25	195
10	27
10:2–4	687
10:6–8	687
10:8	688
10:9	688
10:15–18a	687
10:16	189
10:19	538 n. 43
10:22–23	688

10:22–29	687	20	523 n. 20
10:24	689	20:13	538 n. 44
10:30	538 n. 43	21:20	538 n. 44
11:1	538 n. 43	22	664
11:2	538 n. 43	22:1	538 n. 43
11:12–13	689	22:2	714
12:1	257	22:9–18	259
12:2	838	22:17	663
12:3	814, 838	22:20	538 n. 44, 585
12:4	529 n. 14		n. 26
12:6	529 n. 14, 780	23:1	538 n. 44
12:6–7	779	24:15	538 n. 43
12:7	663	24:30	538 n. 43
12:10	538, 538 n. 43	25:2–4	687
12:10–20	313	25:3	690
12:11	538	25:13–16a	687
12:14–15	538	27:37	628 n. 39
12:16	538 n. 43	27:42	585 n. 26
12:20	518	28:1	518
13:2	530 n. 19	28:6	352
13:7	529 n. 14, 538	28:10–22	782, 792 n. 68
	n. 43	28:13	529 n. 14
14:1	538 n. 44	28:45	352
14:13	529 n. 14	28:46	352
14:18	529 n. 14	29:14	836
15:1	258	29:31	383
15:5	257	30:24	383
15:6	257, 258 n. 4	30:27	628 n. 39
15:7	258 n. 4, 261	31:22	585 n. 26
15:16	188, 804, 806	32:28–29	352
15:16–21	189	32:29	351, 352
15:21	188	33:18–20	775, 779
16:1	534	34	314
16:3–4	535	34:16	824
16:5	535	34:21–22	824
16:6	536	35:1–15	782
16:7	535 n. 33	35:9	788, 790–792
17:1	538 n. 44	35:9–15	792 n. 68, 793
18:2	529 n. 14	35:9ff.	791
18:3	628 n. 39	35:10	790
18:8b	527, 529, 529	35:11	352, 790
	n. 14	35:12	790
19:17	538 n. 43	35:14–15	791
19:29	538 n. 43	35:15	792
19:34	538 n. 44	35:16–20	383

35:18	783	1:10	371
35:22	390	1:17	518, 518 n. 13,
35:22–26	383		521
36:4–5	687	2:1	530, 534
36:11–13a	687	2:2	534
36:12a	808	2:2a	531
36:20–28	687	2:2b	531, 534
36:25	690	2:3	534
36:31	690	2:3a	531
36:31–43	687	2:3b–4	531
36:39	690	2:5	532, 534
38:1–10	687	2:6	532, 534
38:13	585 n. 26	2:7	532, 534
40:3	529 n. 14	2:8a	533
45:1	529 n. 14	2:8b	533
45:16	168	2:9	534
46:7	455, 457	2:9a	533
46:7–11	454	2:9b	533
46:8	455	2:10	529 n. 17
46:8–27	457	2:10a	533–534
46:12	687	2:10b	534
46:28	457	2:11	528, 530 n. 20
47:29–30	806	2:11–25	528
48:3	790, 792	2:11b–14	528
48:3–4	790	2:15a	528
48:20	838	2:15b	528
48:21	806	2:16	530 n. 20
48–49	806	2:16–22	534
49	621	2:23–25	532 n. 26
49:1	795 n. 1, 806	3:1	528, 532 n. 2
49:4	390	3:5	583
49:5–7	391	3:15	838
49:8–12	621	4	678
49:9–10	623, 628, 631	4:1–3	534 n. 31
49:10	619 n. 3, 623,	4:5	585 n. 26
	626 n. 29, 629	4:25	678
49:29	807	5:1–5	534 n. 32
49:33	806	5:2	534 n. 32
50:3	755 n. 1	5:3	534 n. 32
50:22–23	806	5:4	534 n. 32
50:23	804	5:6	534 n. 32
		5:10	534 n. 32
Exodus (Exod)		6:2–8	745
1:5	538	6:23	196
1:6	525 n. 2	6:25	19

7:6	518	21:28–29	297
7:15	819	21:29	230
12:1–20	745	21:31	230
12:15	217 n. 17	21:32	230
12:18–20	745	21:35	230
12:35	518, 518 n. 13	21:37	231
12:49	752	22:3	230
13:6	217	22:4	231, 231 n. 84,
13:9	60		232
13:16	60	22:9	230
13:21	353	22:23	843
14:13	187	22:27	376, 829 n. 6,
14:19	353		831
15	745	22:29	297
15:1	352	23:2	419
15:7	367 n. 2	23:4	230
15:20–21	351	23:22	813
15:21	352	23:23	188–189
17:14	796	23:26	757
17:14–16	809 n. 44	23:32	201
17:15	818 n. 26	23:32–33	194, 201
18:6	823 n. 43	24	48, 217, 678,
18:9	824		678 n. 15
18:25	100	24:7	217, 230
18:27	823 n. 43	24:8	48
19	523 n. 20, 551,	24:16	186
	559, 561	25	355
20	232, 236, 450	25:1–27:19	744
20:1	236	25:1–31:11	745
20:4	60	27:20–21	744
20:5	233, 804	28	744
20:8	60	28:1	196
20:10	67 (LXX), 68,	28:30	195, 201 n. 40
	233	29	362
20:11	60, 68, 234	29:20–21	74, 80
20:14–17	233	29:21	48, 81 n. 30
20:16	233	29:38–46	744
20:17	64, 233, 237	29:42b	752
20:(21)24	218	29:42b–43	750
20:21	236–237	30	49
20:21b	450	30:12–13	47–48
20:24	779	31	745
21:10–11	742	31:6	517 n. 13
21:19	297	31:11	517 n. 13
21:28	230	31:12–17	745

32	48–49	4:7	458
32:2–5	793	4:8	458–459
32:8	48 n. 18	4:9	458
32:19	664	6:7–12	743
32:20	47–48, 48	6:12–13aαβ	743
	n. 17	6:12–18aα	743
32:25–9	314	7:11	742
32:26–28	50	7:11–21	743
32:29	50	7:18	257, 258 n. 4
32:35	48 n. 18	7:22–27	743
33	50, 52	7:28–36	743
33:7	45, 52, 54	8:4	517 n. 13
34	355, 355 n. 30	8:5	517 n. 13
34:6–7a	751	8:8	201 n. 40
34:7	804	8:9	517 n. 13
34:12	193–194, 201	8:30	48
34:12–16	201	8:33	755 n. 1
34:15	194	8–9	362
34:29	722 n. 58	9:6	517 n. 12
35	355	10:10–11	743
35:1	517 n. 12	11:10–38	743
35:1–3	745	11:43–45	743, 750
35:2	233, 745	12	299, 523 n. 20
35:3	745	13:54	518
35:4–39:43	745	14	358 n. 37
35–40	764	14:10	358
38:8	772	14:19–20	358
38:25–26	47	14:31	358
39	523 n. 20	15:21–23	135
40:2	360	15:31	298
40:17	360, 764	16	523 n. 20
		16:1	45 n. 6
Leviticus (Lev)		16:2	744
1:3–5a	750	16:29	742, 752
1:6	750	16:29–34a	744, 750
1:9	750	16:31	742, 745
2:2–3	361	16:34	742
2:9–13	361	16:34a	744
3:1–17	361	17	742
3:16b–17	743, 750	17:3–4	750
4:3	744	17:3–7	743
4:3–9	458	17:4	257, 258 n. 4
4:4	458	17:6	743
4:5	458	17:11	743, 751
4:6	458	17:15	752

18:1–5	741	23	356 n. 30
18:2b–5	741	23:1–3	745
18:6–23	741, 749	23:2aα–3	750
18:12–14	132	23:2aβ–3	742
18:13	467	23:3	70, 745
18:22	741	23:4–38	742, 750
18:24–30	741, 749, 752	23:7–8	359 n. 40
18:26	741, 752	23:9–14	359
18:27	741	23:12	359
18:29	741	23:21	359 n. 40
19	830	23:24–25	359 n. 40
19:2	751	23:27–28	359 n. 40
19:3	745	23:32	745
19:3–4	742	23:35–36	359 n. 40
19:5–8	741	23:37–38	748
19:11–18	751	23:38	745
19:12a	742	23:40	756 n. 13
19:16	829 n. 6	23:40–43	361 n. 48
19:16b	830	23:42–43	742, 750
19:17	251, 845	24:1–4	744
19:18	251, 749	24:4	742
19:19	132	24:16	752
19:30	745	24:22	752
19:33–34	741	25:1	742
19:33–36	741	25:1–24	742
19:34	749, 752	25:4	745
19:35–36	741	25:5–6	742
20:7–8	741	25:30	755 n. 1
20:8	745	25:42	47
20:9–21	741	25:47	47
20:10–21	749	25:53	47
20:22	749	26:1–2	742
20:22–26	741	26:3–28	750
20:25–26	744, 750	26:13	745
21:7	78	26:20	847
21:8	745	26:33b–35	742
21:10	744	26:46	742–743
21:10–15	80 n. 27	27	742
21:15	745		
21:23	745	*Numbers* (Num)	
21:24	742, 750	1:1–3	663
22:16	745	2	388, 390
22:29–30	742	2:3–31	384
22:32	741, 745	2:33	517 n. 13

2:34	517 n. 13, 518	15:4−12	357
3:3−31	387	15:13	752
3:5−10	746	15:24	358 n. 37
3:5−15a	747	15:29	752
3:11−13	745−746, 750	15:30	752
3:14−40	746	15:37−41	747, 751
3:20−22	747	16:30	847
3:40−51	746, 750	16:32	847
3:41aα	746	18:12−13	360
3:45b	746	18:27	257, 258 n. 4
5:1−3	136	19	523 n. 20
5:1−4	746	19:10b	748
6:5	755 n. 1	21:13	215 n. 2
6:24−26	13	21:18	364
6:24−27	9	21:32	188
6:25	91	22	536, 549
7	744	22:1	536
8	744	22:2	536
8:1−4	744	22:2−24:25	807 n. 36
8:14	746	22:6	807
8:14−19	750	22:11	807
8:15b−19	746	22:13	536
8:21	431	22:14	536
9:1−8	747	22:15	549
9:9−14	747	22:30	536
9:17−18	186	22:31	536
10:9	23 n. 4, 24	22:33	536
10:29	823 n. 43	23	549
10:29−32	822	23:2	549
10:32	823	23:7	536
11:15	367 n. 2	23:8	840 n. 22
12:12	367 n. 2	23:9	820
13:1	215 n. 2	23:10	807
13:1−17a	747	23:11	807, 838
13:2	747	23:13	536
14:18	804	23:15	536
14:26−38	747	23:18	536
14:28	549	23:24	807
14:35	747	23:25	807
14:36	549	24:1	536, 807
14:37	549	24:7	619 n. 3
14:43	549	24:8−9	807
15	747	24:10	807, 838
15:4−10	358	24:14	795 n. 1

24:14[b]	808	32:39	188
24:15–17	317, 329	33:50–56	748
24:15–25	808	34:17	186
24:17	330, 333, 619	35:1–8	748
	n. 3, 626 n. 29	35:9–29	748
24:17–22	807	35:11–12	736
24:20	808	35:11–36	748
24:25	536, 807	35:25	737
25	9	35:28	737
25:1–13	261 n. 7	46	748
25:6–13	314		
25:6–15	807 n. 40	*Deuteronomy* (Deut)	
25:13	193, 792	1:1	548
25:16–18	807 n. 40	1:7	708–709
26	523 n. 20	1:8	546
26:1–30:17	807 n. 40	1:17	543
26:19	808 n. 40	1:20	543
27:15–22	186	1:21	544, 546
27:18	187	1:26	546
27:19–23	187	1:27	543
27:21	194–195,	1:28	543
	202–204	1:31	546
28:2b	748	1:35	546
28:3–8	744	1:36	542
28:6	358 n. 37	1:41	546
28:12–14	358	1:42	547
28:24	358 n. 37	1:43	547
28:26–31	359	1:44	546
28:27	358 n. 37, 359	2	523 n. 20
28:30	359	2:1	546
28–29	356 n. 30,	2:6	543
	357–359	2:9	543
29:1–6	360	2:11	544, 547
29:2	358 n. 37	2:13	543
29:13	358 n. 37	2:14	543, 544
29:39	748	2:14	544
30:16	548	2:15	547
30:17	743	2:16	544
31:1	807 n. 40	2:26	546, 547
31:5	548	2:27	544, 547
31:8	548, 807	2:29	542
31:9	548	2:30	546
31:13	548	2:37	542
31:40	807	3:2	546
32:27	517 n. 12	3:6	544, 546

3:13	546	5:18–21	233
3:15	546	5:20	233, 233 n. 88
3:16	542	5:21	233, 544, 546
3:18	541, 544	5:22	61–62, 233
3:21	546	5:22–26	236
3:25	708–709, 710	5:23	59, 64, 233
	n. 17, 715–717	5:23–6:1	65
3:26	710 n. 17	5:24	59, 66, 67
4:1	547		n. 18, 548
4:10	542	5:25	62, 66, 236
4:11	61–62, 233	5:26	62, 66
4:11–13	61	5:27	233, 544
4:12	61	5:27a	62
4:12a	61	5:27b	62
4:12–13	63	5:27–28	236
4:13	61	5:28	64, 233, 237,
4:19	541		546
4:25	542–543, 806	5:28–29	236
4:29	544	5:29	450, 548
4:30	546, 795 n. 1,	5:30	59, 237
	806	5:31	62, 64
4:32	542	5:31–33	62
4:41	541	5:32	63–64, 542
4:47	544	5:32–33	64–65
5	232	5:32–36:1	63
5:1	60, 63, 67	6:1	62, 64–65
5:1b	68	6:1–2	63–64
5:1–5	236	6:2	64–65, 67,
5:2	63		542, 544
5:2–3	63	6:4	548
5:3	66	6:6	61
5:5	63, 66	6:7	544, 548
5:6	63	6:8	60, 544
5:6–21	60	6:9	546
5:8	233	6:12	544, 546
5:9	233, 804	6:15	544, 548
5:11	63	6:17	548
5:12	60, 67, 237,	6:18	542, 548
	517 n. 13	6:20	542, 546
5:14 (LXX)	67	6:21	544
5:14	67, 233–234	6:22	544, 548
5:14–15	234	6:24	544
5:14b–15	60, 68	6:25	263
5:15	68, 517 n. 13	7	355, 355 n. 30
5:16	63, 517 n. 13	7:1	188

7:1–6	201	11:23	542
7:2	189, 194, 201	11:24	542, 708–709
7:10	544, 548	11:26	547
7:11	235	11:29	542
7:12	544, 548	11:30	544, 779, 780
7:15	251	11:31–12:7	763, 764
7:19	544, 546	11:31–12:28	765
7:20	543	11:32	547
7:21	544, 548	12:2–4	763
7:22	544	12:3	374 n. 31, 544,
7:24	544		546–547
8:1	235	12:5	546
8:2	548	12:6	542–544
8:7–10	312	12:8–12	761–762
8:12	544, 547	12:10	544
8:14	542	12:11	186, 762
8:19	546	12:12	542
9:3	543–544	12:16	675 n. 2
9:8	50, 548	12:17	542–543
9:11	543–544	12:26	542
9:12	48 n. 18, 544,	12:29	542
	546	12:30	194
9:15	546	12:30	470
9:16	48 n. 18, 544,	13	217, 830
	548	13:2	544
9:21	48, 541–543	13:2–6	202 n. 41
9:25	544	13:5	544, 548
9:26	548	13:6	544
10:4	541, 543	13:10	544
10:7	541, 543	13:12	546
10:8	753	13:13–16	830
10:11	542	13:14	544
11	232	13:15	547
11:3	542, 544	13:16	542–544, 546
11:6	542	13:17	544
11:7	542	13:18	544
11:8	235	14:8	544
11:10	544	14:14	544
11:10–17	43 n. 4	14:20	542
11:11	546	14:21	546
11:17	542–543, 847	14:28	544
11:18	542	15:2	40, 547
11:19	63, 68, 547	15:3	543, 546
11:21	542	15:4	542
11:22	547	15:5	544

15:6	542	19:11	547
15:9	542	19:12	547
15:10	548	19:13	835
15:11	547–548	19:14	842
15:12	548	19:15	547
15:15	547	19:17	545
15:18	333	19:18	545, 548
15:20	547	19:19	548
16:3	546	19:20	545–546
16:6	546	19:21	548
16:8	217 n. 17	20:1	547
16:9	359	20:2–4	23 n. 4
16:14	544	20:3	545, 547
16:15	548	20:4	547
16:18	544, 546	20:7	547–548
16:20	544	20:9	547
17	47	20:10	542
17:3	79	20:10–18	195
17:5	79, 542,	20:12	546
	547–548	20:14	544, 545–546
17:7	546	20:15	195
17:9	544	20:15–17	201
17:10	543	20:16	195, 548
17:11	63, 547	20:16–17	189
17:14	542, 545	20:16–18	201
17:14–20	414	20:17	188, 542, 546
17:15	545	20:17–18	194
17:17	133	20:18	545
17:19	545–546, 828	21:2	546
17:20	545–546	21:3	547
18	450	21:5	545
18:1	753	21:6	545
18:3	547	21:8	835
18:4	360	21:13	548
18:5	547	21:15–17	133
18:7	542	21:16	545
18:13	547	21:17	542, 546
18:15	326–328, 766	21:18	547
18:15–16	236	21:20	545
18:18	326, 450, 546	21:21	576
18:18–19	236, 317, 328	21:22–23	250
19	737	21:23	545
19:3	841 n. 26	22:1	230, 543
19:8	544	22:2	548
19:10	835	22:3	542, 545

22:4	230, 545	25:19	796, 809
22:5	47, 547	26:3	548
22:6	544, 545	26:4	543
22:9	546	26:6	545–546
22:13–21	47	26:8	548
22:14	548	26:10	542
22:18	545	26:12	546
22:20	546	26:13	544
22:21	547	26:15	191, 548
22:25	546, 548	27:1	518
22:27	545, 547	27:1–8	776
23:4	546	27:4	218, 545, 779
23:5	545	27:4–8	764
23:5–6	807	27:5	544
23:10	546	27:6	542
23:10–15	746	27:8	542–543
23:12	547	27:10	545
23:13	542–544	27:12	547
23:15	544	27:12–13	390
23:16–17	195	27:20	390
23:20	545	27:22	545, 546, 548
23:25–26	47	28:1	543
24:1–3	798	28:4	545–546
24:1–4	133	28:6	542
24:2	543	28:7	543
24:3	545	28:8	542, 548
24:4	544–546, 548	28:11	545
24:8	545, 548	28:13	545
24:12	545	28:14	63
24:13	545	28:15	547
24:13c	263	28:16	542
24:15	545, 546, 548	28:18	545
24:18	545	28:20	542
24:19	542, 544–545	28:22	545
24:19–21	47	28:28	545
24:20	546	28:32	545
25:3	542	28:34	548
25:5–10	134 n. 23	28:35	543
25:6	546, 548	28:39	545
25:7	548	28:40	545
25:9	545	28:41	542
25:11	545–546	28:43	545, 548
25:13	542	28:44	545
25:15	547	28:48	542, 545
25:16	542, 548	28:52	547–548

28:53	545, 548	31:27	805
28:56–57	545	31:29	795 n. 1, 805
28:58	545	32	551, 561
28:60	546	32:5	542
28:61	542	32:7	547
28:65	545–547	32:8	788
28:68	544	32:11	543
29:1	548	32:12	820
29:3	548	32:17	548
29:13	545–546, 548	32:19	547
29:16	548	32:24	548
29:18	548	32:25	543
29:19	545	32:27	548
29:20	545	32:29	543
29:21	542, 545, 548,	32:38	548
	799	32:42	733
29:23	544–545, 547	32:43	543, 548, 788
29:25	544	33	449
29:26	545	33:2	542
29:28	548	33:8	201 n. 40
30:3	542	33:8–11	192, 314, 317,
30:5	325		329, 391, 448
30:6	545	33:10	753
30:9	542	33:12	191, 193, 199
30:10	542, 548	33:12c	192, 193
30:15	542		n. 29
30:16	544, 547	33:12d	192
30:18	235, 542	33:13	543
31:1	806	33:17	543
31:3–13	806	33:27	543
31:6	543	34:1	662
31:8	543	34:3	547
31:9	543	34:4	542, 662
31:10	827 n. 2	34:5–7	806
31:10–11	827	34:7	543
31:10–13	361 n. 48, 827	34:9	187
	n. 2		
31:13	235	*Joshua* (Josh)	
31:14–16	806	1–23	764
31:15	548	1:4	709 n. 11,
31:17	545		716
31:19	547	1:17	584
31:20	548	2:6	805 n. 32
31:21	543	2:12–17	772
31:25	542	2:27–36	772

10:38	575 n. 9, 576 n. 12	24:33	789, 793
		30:4	663
10:43	575 n. 9, 576 n. 12, 579, 581, 584–585	33:18	776
		35:8	776
11:3	572	*Judges* (Judg)	
11:15	584	1:16	824 n. 46
11:17	709 n. 11	1:21	188, 191, 200
12:7	709 n. 11	1:29	193
12:16	197	2:1	786–788
13:5	709 n. 11, 712	2:1–5	770
13:6	709 n. 11	2:3–4	244
13:22	807	3:3	709 n. 11
14:1	186, 203	3:15	564
14:5	584	3:20	563–564
15:63	188, 200	3:24	377
17:4	186, 203	4:11	824 n. 46
18:1	186, 196–197, 197 n. 35, 198, 200, 766, 770	4:21	824 n. 47
		5:14	784 n. 51
		5:31	846
18:1–10	764, 789	6:25–32	766
18:6	766	6:32	374
18:8	197, 766	7:1	374
18:10	197, 766	8:29	374
18:12	783 n. 49	8:35	374
18:28	191	9:1	374
18–22	768	9:2	374
19	194	9:5	374
19:51	186, 196, 200, 203, 764, 766	9:15	709 n. 11
		9:16	374
20	736	9:19	374
21:1	186	9:24	374
21:1–2	196	9:25	585 n. 26
21:2	197	9:28	374
22:2	663	9:47	585 n. 26
22:10–12	663	9:57	374
22:29	764, 766	11:1	845
24	764–765	11:12	840 n. 22
24:1	771, 788	13:10b–11a	565
24:1–28	779	13:11	563–564
24:9–10	807, 809 n. 44	13:16	565
24:25	788	16:6	566
24:25–26	771	16:6–8a	565
24:32	775	16:7	566

16:21	568	4:27	774
16:21b–23a	567	4:29	774
16:22–23	568	5:6	377
16:23	564	5:8	198 n. 37
16:26	568, 841	5:12	377
16:29	841	6:4	377
18:30–31	773	6:5	377
19:10–12	188	7:6	765
20:18	784	7:17	765
20:23	786	8:19	79
20:26	784	9:12–13	765
20:26–28	197 n. 35, 788	9:19–24	765
20:27	197 n. 35	9:21	625 n. 25
20:27–28	789, 793	10:3	784
21:13–24	361	10:5	593
21:19–20	360	10:8	765
		10:19	625 n. 25
Ruth		10:20	625 n. 25
1:8–19	824	10:21	625 n. 25
1:16–17	813	12	764
4:2	419	12:11	374
4:18–22	187	13:3	593
		13:4	593
1 Samuel (1 Sam)		13:5	783 n. 49
1:6	812 n. 6	13:7	784 n. 51
1:9	766–767	13:8–14	765
1:17	836	14:15	784 n. 51
1:24	766	14:23	783 n. 49
1–3	766	14:32–34	675 n. 2
2:1	819, 819 n. 26,	14:33	597
	819 n. 28	14:47	838
2:8	340	14:48	809
2:10	115	15:3	809
2:17	369	15:6	824 nn. 46–47
2:22	773	15:7	809
2:22b	772	15:12	585 n. 26
2:28	625 n. 25	15:17	625 n. 25
2:35	15, 193	15:33	596
3:3	766	16:21	846
3:11–14	772	17	737
3:13	367 n. 2, 376	17:11	575 n. 9
3:15	766	18:29	846
4	774	19:19	585 n. 26
4:7	774	20:8	340
4:21–22	774	20:16b	370

21:2–10	767	7	622
21:5–7	746	7:7	625 nn. 26, 28
22:9–3	767	7:11	298
22:10	201	7:11–14	330
23:4	201	7:12	755
23:7	585 n. 26	7:14	330, 333
24:4	377	7:16	619 n. 3, 841
25:22	370	7:23	818
25:31	441	9:6	374
27:4	585 n. 26	9:10	374
27:10	824 n. 46	9:11	374
27:12	831	9:12	374
28:6	195	9:13	374
30:29	824 n. 46	10:17	585 n. 26
		11:1	752
2 Samuel (2 Sam)		11:1–27	368
1:1	446	11:11	746
1:17–27	807	11:21	374
1:18	807	12:1–14	368
1:21	797 n. 14	12:9	372
1–11:1	625 n. 28	12:12	369
2:8	374–375, 375	12:14	367–369
	n. 35	12:25	192
2:10	374	14:11	369
2:12	374	14:22	444, 448
2:15	374, 375, 375	14:23	369
	n. 35	14:30	445
2:22	766	15:2	625 n. 26
3:7	374	15:3	444
3:8	374	15:8	441, 444
3:14	374	15:10	625 n. 26
3:15	374	16:1	374
3:37	575 n. 9	16:4	374
4:1	375, 575 n. 9	16:12	376
4:2	375	16:30	369
4:4	374	18:14	625 n. 26
4:5	374	18:17	575 n. 9
4:8	374	19:1	585 n. 26
4:12	374–376	19:10	625 n. 26
5:1	625 nn. 26, 28,	19:20	258 n. 4
	836	19:24	374
5:6	188, 200	19:25	374
5:6–9	188	19:30	374
5:7	187–188	20:1	367 n. 2, 376,
6:12	585 n. 26		840 n. 22

20:14	625 n. 26	11:16	575 n. 9
21:7	374	11:31	625 n. 25
21:8	374	11:32	625 n. 25
21:11	585 n. 26	11:35	625 n. 25
21:15–16	602	11:36	625 n. 25
22	87	12:16	377
22:2	188, 599–600	12:20	625 n. 25
22:49	352	12:21	625 n. 25
24:2	625 n. 26	12:30	784
24:11	752	13:2	187
24:14	337	13:3	187
24:18–24	188	13:34	784
		14:16	784
1 Kings (1 Kgs)		14:21	762
1:51	585 n. 26	15:20	433
2	765	15:22	602
2:7 (LXX)	650	15:26	506
2:13–21:29	625 n. 28	15:27	575 n. 9
2:28	586	16:7	506
2:29	585 n. 26, 586	16:17	575 n. 9
2:41	585 n. 26	18:4	344, 447
3:3–4	767	18:19	375, 752
3:7	190	18:30–39	766
5:18–19	762	18:31	625 n. 25
5:20	709 n. 11, 716	21:10	369 n. 12, 831
5:22	189	21:13	369 n. 12, 831
5:23	709 n. 11	22:6	752
5:24	189		
5:28	709 n. 11	*2 Kings* (2 Kgs)	
7:2	709 n. 11, 713	2:14–16	300
	n. 26, 714	4:28	195
	n. 35, 716, 718	6:13	585 n. 26
7:13–51	773	6:24–31	798
8:1–11	773	6:28–30	798
8:4	188	8:7	585 n. 26
8:15	625 n. 25	8:12	831
8:17	189	9:14	575 n. 9
8:62	575 n. 9	10:31	804
8:65 (LXX)	575 n. 9	11:4	593
9:3	711	14:6	290
9:19	709 n. 11	14:9	707 n. 5, 709
10:17	709 n. 11		n. 11, 713
10:21	709 n. 11		n. 28
11:13	625 n. 25	15:44	595

29:22	190	*Ezra*	
29:30	186	2:63	201 n. 40, 202 n. 41
2 Chronicles (2 Chr)		2:70	575 nn. 9–10
1:3	767	3:7	718 n. 41
1:5–6	767, 789	3:8–11	362
2:6	189	4:3	300
2:7	189, 709 n. 11	7:9	360
		7:10	470
2:15	709 n. 11	8:25	575 nn. 9–10
5:5	188	10:5	575 nn. 9–10
5:5	773	10:17	360
6:42	340		
6:7	189	*Nehemiah* (Neh)	
6:8	189	6:14	800 n. 22
6:9	190	7:65	195, 201 n. 40, 202 n. 41
7:6	575 n. 9		
7:7–9	362	7:72	575 nn. 9–10
7:8	575 n. 9	8:1–8	361 n. 48
8:6	709 n. 11	8:8	272, 354 n. 27
8:14	89	8:14–18	361 n. 48
9:16	709 n. 11	9:7–8	259
9:20	709 n. 11	9:25f.	337
10:3	575 nn. 9–10	9:35	337
10:16	377	10:35–40	360
12:1	575 nn. 9–10	12:24	89
13:4	575 nn. 9–10	12:44–47	361
13:15	575 nn. 9–10	13:2	807
15:5	186	13:10	361
16:4	433	13:14	340
17:7–9	575	13:31	186, 361
20:14–17	752		
24:20–22	287	*Esther* (Esth)	
25:18	707 n. 5	1:5	755 n. 1
25:18	709 n. 11	9:28	838
29:17	360		
30:27	191	*Job*	
31:19	361	1:2	804
31:4–9	361	1:5	369 n. 12
31:5	360	1:11	369 n. 12
32:32	340	1–2	551
34:22	594	2:5	369 n. 12
35:26	340	2:9	369 n. 12
36:16	627 n. 35	3:13	755 n. 4

5:21	655	3:4	646, 653
5:22	655	3:5	646
7:20	367 n. 2	3:6	653
8:7	804	3:6a–6bα	646
9:22	835	3:6b–7	646
10:12	345	3:8	656
13:24	259 n. 4	3:8a	646
14:2	757	3:8b–c	646
14:12	755 n. 4	3:9	646, 652, 659
14:18	840	3:9a	659
15:32	756	3:9b	659
16:6	840 n. 22	4:2	657
18:5–6	801	5	551
18:17	838	5:7	335
18:17–19	801	5:10	297
19:11	259 n. 4	6:2–5	297–298
19:15	844 n. 36	6:3	836
19:19	335	6:4	656
21:12	648	6:6	297
24:9	843	7:11	653
24:24	757	7–9	88
29:17	846	10:3	369
30:31	648	11:1–2	297
31:14	345 n. 27	12:1	297
33:10	259 n. 4	12:3–4	471
33:21	836	12:6	846
38:7	94, 96	12:7	297
39:28	188	13:2–3	297
42:12	530	13:5	297
42:12–13	804	16:3	251, 297
42:16	804	17:1	297
		17:1a	251
Psalms (Ps)		17:36	653
1:1	297	18	87, 599
1:3	840	18:3	88, 188
2:1	297	18:4	88
2:1–3	727	18:7–9	95
2:7	725	18:18	88
2:7–9	727	18:19	88
2–3	646	18:43	599 n. 21
3:1	649–650	18:49	352
3:2	651	19:3	653
3:2–3	646	19:5	845
3:3	658	21:29	659

23:1	659	61:13	659
23:10	652	62:1	650
24:1	649	62:11	839
24:2	841	65:3	651
24:5	258	67:1	209
25:12	837	67:21	659
26:12	299	68:1	209
29:5	709 n. 11, 712	68:5	657
	n. 24, 717	68:20	91 n. 16
29:6	709 n. 11, 712	68:36	91 n. 16
	n. 25	72:13	657
30:1	209	72:16	709 n. 11,
31:11	836		712 n. 24
32:2	258 n. 4, 263	72:18–20	91 n. 16
33:1	649	73:22	656
34:7	657	75:5	656
34:17	801, 838	77:13	335
34:19	657	77:18	256
34:19a	657	78	774
37:1	837	78:3–6	799
37:7	473 n. 24	78:60	766, 774, 787
37:23	840		n. 60
37:37–38	800	78:68–70	774
38:4	836	79:2b–3	281
39:6	656	81:8	656
40:4	653	82:3	843
40:7	657	83:1	209
41:14	91 n. 16	83:12	653
43:27	656	87:1	209
45:12	652	88:1	209
46:10	653, 659	88:19	653, 659
47:14	799	88:48	657
48:1	209	89:15	93 n. 22
48:3	156 n. 17, 711	89:53	91 n. 16
48:14	799	91:15	818, 820
51:3	337	92	40
51:4	556	92:1	209
52:9	839	92:3	717
55:1	649–650	92:13	707 n. 2, 709
55:9	656		n. 11, 712
56:1	650		n. 24
57:7	658	92:13–14	710 n. 17
58:1	649	93:18	653
58–59	551	94:6	843
59:2	649	95:7	41

95:7–8	41	139:21–22	814
95:11	41	140:13	846
97:2	93 n. 22	141:1	650
98:1	209	144:16	656
102:10	835	145:9	340
103:13	340	150	463
103:15	653	151 (LXX)	649
103:7	335	151:1 (LXX)	648
104:16	709 n. 11, 712 n. 24	151:3 (LXX)	649
105:3	54 n. 32	*Proverbs* (Prov)	605–618
106:20	367 n. 2	1	609
106:30–31	261 n. 7	1:1–6	299
106:39	335	1:10	607
106:40	341	1:11	834
106:48	91 n. 16	1:18	835
107:18	341	1:22	607
108	552	1:27	56 n. 39
108:1	209	1:32	607
108:3	657	2:16	844
109:2	801	2:22	607
109:6	801	3:2	335
109:7	801	3:8	835
109:12–13	808	3:12	845
109:13	801–802	3:25	607
109:15	838	3:31	837
110	333	3:33	607
110:3	619 n. 3	3:35	607
117:20	659	4:14	607
118	552	4:19	607
118:114	653	4:22	836
118:116	653	4:26	841 n. 26
118:117	653	5:20	844
118:161	657	6:17	835
119:163	335	6:24	845
126:1	657	6:26	845
132:13	837	7:5	844–845
135	552	7:10	845
135:7	92	7:12	299
135:13	838	9:7	607
135:21	91 n. 16	10	552, 609
138:20–139:9a	553	10:3	607
138–140	552	10:6	607
139:5	138 n. 35	10:7	607, 837
139:9b–140:5a	557	10:11	607

10:15	607	24:1	837
10:16	607	24:7	612
10:20	607	24:8	612
10:24	607	24:21	613
10:25	607	24:22	612
10:27	607	24:11	615
10:28	607	24:12	615
10:30	607	24:13	615
10:32	607	24:14	615
11:4	607	24:19	837
11:5	840	24:20	801
11:7	607	24:23	614
11:8	607	24:23–34	614
11:9	607	24:24	614
11:10	607	24:25	614
11:18	607	24:26	614
11:19	607	24:27	614
11:23	607	24:28–29	614
11:26	838	24:30–34	614
11:28	839	24–31	608–618
11:31	607	25	609–610, 616
12:4	839	25:1	617
12:6	835	25:1–8	617
12:12	835	25:2	609, 617
13:9	801	25:3	609, 617
13:17	346	25:4	617
14:8	343, 841	25:5–6	609
14:29	337	25:5–8	617
14:30	836, 839	25:7	609
15:8	298	25:15	337
15:18	337	27:2	844 n. 36
15:25	843	27:5	845
16:9	841	28:5	54 n. 32
16:32	337	29	611, 617
19:21	841	29:10	611
19:25	343	29:25	617
20:24	840	29:25–27	617
21:29	841	29:26	617
22:14	844	29:27	610, 617
22:17	844	30	609, 614, 617
22:28	841–842	30	618
23:10	841–843	30:1	613
23:18	803, 803 n. 27	30:1–14	613–614
23:27	844	30:2	613
24	612–616	30:3	613

30:4	613	31:13–18	611
30:5	613	31:14	798
30:6	613	31:15	611
30:7	613	31:15a	798
30:8	613	31:15b	798
30:9	613	31:16	798
30:10	613	31:19	611, 798
30:11	614	31:20	611
30:11–14	614	31:21	798
30:12	614	31:23	611, 798
30:13	614	31:24–25	611
30:14	614, 846–847	31:25	798
30:15	616	31:26	611
30:15–33	616	31:27	611
30:16	616	31:28	611
30:17	616		
30:18	616	*Qohelet* (Qoh)	
30:19	616	9:16	338
30:20	616		
30:21	616	*Song of Solomon* (Song)	
30:22	616	1:17	718
30:23	616	3:9	709, 713, 717,
30:24	616		721, 723
30:25	616	4:6	714
30:26	616	4:8	709, 710 n. 17,
30:27	616		713, 723
30:28	616	4:11	710, 710
30:29	616		n. 16, 714,
30:30	616		719–721,
30:31	616		723
30:32	616	4:13	720
30:33	616	4:13–15	720
31	609–611, 617	4:14	720
31:1–9	610, 616–617	4:15	709, 713, 713
31:2–3	617		n. 31, 720,
31:4–5	617		723
31:6–7	617	5:5	710
31:8–9	617	5:15	712 n. 24, 713,
31:9	609		713 n. 31
31:10–12	617	7:3	836
31:10–31	609–611, 617	7:5	707 n. 2, 710,
31:11	798		713, 713
31:11–12	611		n. 31, 717,
31:12	798		722–723
31:13	798	7:9	723

Isaiah (Isa)
1:18	710
1:20	733
2:2	795 n. 1, 796 n. 6
2:2–4	809
2:13	708, 713 n. 27, 714 n. 35
5:5	231
5:11–14	472
6	435 n. 13
6:3	90, 93, 94 n. 25, 95
7:2	585 n. 26
7:6	500
7:14	187, 619, 809
7:14ff.	330
8:21	831
9:1–5	619
9:6	810
10:24–11:10	21, 25
10:34	25–26, 707 n. 3, 708, 712 n. 24, 713 n. 714 n. 35, 717
10:34–11:1	3 n. 1
11:1ff.	333
11:3	213
11:4	6, 26, 330, 619 n. 3
14:8	708, 714 n. 35, 715, 755 n. 4
14:19–32	619 n. 3
15:2	446 n. 37
19:18	780
22:18	340
23:15–17	810
24:4	840
24:17	474
26:3	339
26:8	838
28:14–15	472
28:16	299
28:22	472

29:17	709 n. 12, 712 nn. 24–25, 714–715, 717
30:10–11	471
30:12	839
32:6	472 n. 19
32:7	472 n. 22
34:4	840
35:2	709 n. 12, 713 n. 29
36:12	377 n. 43
36–37	669
37:24	709, 713 n. 27, 714, 714 n. 35
38:21–22	735
40:3	56 n. 38, 97, 105, 298, 484, 488
40:4	734
40:7	441
40:7–8	444
40:13	710 n. 17
40:16	709 n. 12, 712 n. 24, 714, 717
41:29	782 n. 47
42:3	344
42:6	441
43:17	755 n. 4
45:2	734
49:15	843
51:1	54 n. 32
54:12	739
54:14	839
55:3	340
57:18	346
58	560–561
58:11	562
58:11–14	552, 561
58:12	562
58:13	39–40, 562
60:5	336
60:13	709 n. 12, 712 nn. 24–25
61:1	332 n. 26, 333
61:1ff.	332 n. 26

63:7	340	23:5–6	803 n. 29
63:9	818, 818 n. 23,	23:20	795 n. 1
	819 n. 26, 820	23:22	335
63:9–10	846	25:1–8	706 n. 11
64:5	840	25:1–13	705
65:20	757	25:5	335
66:3	837	25:9	705, 706 n. 11
66:10	821	25:11	308, 804
66:10–11	821	25:12	755 n. 1
66:20	648	25:13	705–706
69:20	843	25:15–38	704–705
		25:18	705
Jeremiah (Jer)		25:29	705
1:1–11	299	25:34	755 n. 7
2:11	367 n. 2	26	704
3:24–25	785	26:13	335
4:18	335	28 (LXX)	92 n. 21
5:31	803	29:1	705
7:5	335	29:6	804
8:13	840	29:10	308, 481, 755
9:20	847 n. 46		n. 1, 804
9:22–23	703 n. 8	29:10–11	804
9:23–24	115	29:11	803, 803 n. 27,
9:24–25	703 n. 8		803 n. 29
10	91–92	30:2	705
10:12	92	30:24	795 n. 1
10:12–13	90, 92, 92	31:6	803 n. 27
	n. 19, 95–96	31:16–17	803, 803 n. 29
10:13	91 n. 15, 92–93	32:19	335
10:13a	92	33:14–16	803 n. 29
10:16	626 n. 29	33:17–18	15
10:23	841	35:15	335
11:10	842	36:2	706 n. 1
11:13	375	40–44	299
17:10	335	45:1	705
18:11	335	46:1	705
18:14	709 n. 12	48:7	839 n. 17
22:6	707 n. 4, 709	48:47	795 n. 1, 810
	n. 14, 713	49:4	839 n. 17
	n. 27, 714	49:39	795 n. 1, 810
22:15–17	839 n. 18	50:1–51:58	700
22:20	709, 713 n. 27,	50:17	799 n. 20
	714 n. 35	50:21	803
22:23	707 n. 4, 709	50:26	803
22:26	714 n. 35	50:36	371

50:41–43	701	17:3–24	707 n. 5
50:44–46	701	17:23	619 n. 3
51	92	18:5–9	258
51:13	756 n. 11	19:11	626 n. 30
51:15	92	19:14	626 n. 30
51:15–19	701	20:32	629–630
51:16	92	20:37	626 n. 30, 630
51:16a	92		n. 43
51:19	626 n. 29	20:43	335
51:46	337	21:3	621, 624
51:59–64	701	21:10	622
51:60	705	21:11	556, 622
51:63	705	21:13	622
52:12–13	299	21:13–18	622, 624
		21:13–22	622
Lamentations (Lam)		21:14a	622
1:1	299	21:14b–15	624
1:2	846	21:14b–16	622
4:18	755	21:14b–18	622
		21:15	619, 623–626,
Ezekiel (Ezek)			629–631
1:24	92–93	21:15b	621–622,
1:24–25	92		624–626
3:12	94, 94 n. 25	21:15–18	630
3:12–13	92	21:16	624
5:2	755 n. 1	21:17	628, 630
7:2	756 n. 11, 796	21:17–18a	622, 624
	n. 11	21:18	619, 624–626,
7:3	756 n. 11, 796		629–631
	n. 11	21:18b	621–622, 624,
7:21	796 n. 11		627
7:30	796 n. 11	21:19–22a	622
7:34	796 n. 11	21:22b	622
8:17	367 n. 2	21:23–32	628
9:4	800 n. 21	21:24	622
10:3	26	21:26	95
13:10	474, 475	21:30–32	619 n. 3, 631
14:3	342	21:31–32	630
14:22	335	21:32	621, 623–624
14:23	335	21:33	627 n. 34
16:4	836	22:9	830
16:8	3	23:25	802
17:3	138 n. 35, 709	24:2	839
	n. 12, 714	24:14	335
	n. 35, 716–717	25:15	845

27:5	709 n. 12,	*Daniel* (Dan)	
	712 n. 25,	2:4	155 n. 8
	714	2:10	156 n. 17
30:13	624 n. 24	2:28	795
30:18	803	2:41	154 n. 5
31:3	707 n. 5, 709	2:45	156 n. 13
	n. 12, 714	3:9	155 n. 8
	n. 35	4:17	156 n. 13
31:15	708, 714 n. 35	4:31	156 n. 15
31:16	708	5:6	155 n. 9
31:18	340, 755 n. 4	5:10	155 n. 8
32:21	755 n. 4	7	154
32:27	755 n. 4	7:9–10	311
32:30	755 n. 4	7:10	157 n. 19
35:5	796 n. 11	7:13	619 n. 3
36:17	335	7:13–14	492
36:19	335	7:18	154
36:19b	312	7:18–28	157 n. 20
36:20aβ	312	7:27	156 n. 16
36:25	342 n. 20	7–11	152
36:30a	312	9:2	272
36:31a	312	9:24	337, 481
36:33aβ	312	9:25–27	481
37:19	626 n. 30	9:27	492
38:11	10	10:7	155 n. 7
38:16	795 n. 1	10:14	795 n. 1, 796
38:8	795 n. 1		n. 6
38–39	21, 25	11	480
39:3–4	24	11:1–12:3	21, 28
39:9–16	26	11:4	802
40:5	382 n. 10	11:13	186
40–48	318, 381 n. 9	11:30	25
41:18	756 n. 16	11:31	492
41:19	756 n. 16	11–12	25
43:2	92	12	480
43:3	619 n. 3	12:3	294
43:13	382 n. 10	12:12	481, 492
43:18–27	362		
44:15	13, 294	*Hosea* (Hos)	
45:11	47	1:6–2:5	246
47:12	840	2:2	445 n. 32
47:22–23	752	2:7	835
48	388, 390	2:11	360
48:30–35	382, 382 n. 10,	2:17	374 n. 31
	384, 385 n. 19	2–4	246–247, 251

3:5	336, 795 n. 1,	1–2	256
	796 n. 6	1–5	251
4:15	782, 784–785	1–9	247
5:8	782, 784–785,	2:6	839
	785 n. 55	2:9–10	188
5:11	474	2–4	246
6:6	787	4:2	801, 803
6:7	787	4:13	619 n. 3
6:8	787	4:30	802
6:9	787	5:5	782, 785
6:10	787	5:6	788
6–14	247, 251	5:12	839
8:10	619 n. 3	5:23	648–649
10:5	783, 785	6–7	246
10:8	783–785	6–9	256
10:12	473 n. 25	7:13	781
10:15	787	7–9	251
12:5	783, 785	8:2	756 n. 11
12:12	785	9:1–2	802
13	246	9:11	291
14:6	707 n. 3,		
	709 n. 12,	*Obadiah* (Obad)	247, 251
	712 n. 25	1–2	256
14:6–8	715, 717, 724		
14:7	723	*Jonah* (Jon)	
14:7–8	713 n. 27	1:3	245
14:8	709, 723	1:4	245
14:16	714 n. 35	1:1–5,7–8	245
		1:3a	245
Joel		1:3b	245
1:3	799 n. 19	1:6–8,10–16	247
1:6	846	1–4	247, 252, 256
1–2	246–247, 251		
2:2	251	*Micah* (Mic)	
2:3	256	1–5	256
2:23	473 n. 25	1–6	247, 252
3:5	508	1–7	256
4	246, 251	2:11	473, 474
		2:6	467, 474
Amos		3:3	836
1:2–3	247	4:1	795 n. 1
1:3–5	247	4:1–4	809
1:5	626 n. 29	5:1	626 n. 29
1:8	626 n. 29	5:1–2	247

5:1–4	809	1:16	254
5:4	847 n. 46	1–2	243
6:8	343	2:1	255–256
7	247, 252	2:1–2	272
7:2	835	2:1–8a	256
7:4	270 n. 3	2:13–20	256
7:17	336	2:2	486
		2:2ff.	
Nahum (Nah)		2:3	253–254
1:1–14	256	2:3a	486
1:2	251	2:3b	486
1:3–3:14	248	2:4	247, 252,
1:3–6	250		254–256
1:4	709 n. 12, 713	2:4b	244
	n. 28	2:5–11	256
1:7–9	248	2:11	255, 256
1:13f.	256	2:12–13	473
1–3	247, 252	2:15	38, 254
2:1–14	256	2:17	709, 712
2:5–10,13f.	256		n. 24, 713
2:9–11	248		n. 27,
2:11	251		715–717
2:12–13	466	2:18–20	256
2:12–14	250	3	243
2:13	250	3:1–19	256
3:1–3	248	3:3	651
3:1–5	250	3:9	651
3:1–19	256	3:9–15	256
3:3	256	3:10	256
3:4	475	3:13	651
3:6–9	250	3:16	839
3:6–17	256		
3:10–12	250	*Zephaniah* (Zeph)	
3:17	248	1:6	54 n. 33, 448
			n. 34
Habakkuk (Hab)		1–3	246, 256
1:3–13	256	2–3	246
1:5	253	3	252
1:11	254, 256	3:3–5	247
1:14–17	256	3:4	251
1:12	255–256, 367		
	n. 2, 441	*Haggai* (Hag)	
1:13b	254, 472	1:8	718 n. 41
1:15	256	1–2	246, 256

2:9	799	10:6	314 n. 28
2:18–21	247	10:10	709, 713 n. 27,
2:19	247		715, 717
		10–12	247, 252
Zechariah (Zech)		11:1	708, 713 n. 26,
1:1	287		714 n. 35
1:1–4	256	13:7	800 n. 21
1:4	800		
1:7	661	*Malachi* (Mal)	
1–3; 8–9	256	1:10	298
1–8	247	1:13	367 n. 2
2:12	367 n. 2,	2:4–8	314
	661	2:14	37
4:14	328	3:3–6	246
6:14	648	3:13–24	810
7:10	843	3:13–4:6	810
7:12	800	3:22	245
9:9	819 n. 28	3:23	245
9:10	619 n. 3	3:23–24	800
9:11	314 n. 29	3:24	246

(B) New Testament

Matthew (Matt)	563	24:4–8	492
3:2	488	24:9–14	492
3:3	488	24:15–22	492
3:5–6	488	24:23–26	326
3:13	488	24:23–28	492
4:17	488–489	24:29	492
5:17	287	24:30–31	492
5:32	134 n. 22	24:33–34	492
6:11	489	24:36	489
6:34	489		
7:12	287, 749 n. 37	*Mark* (Mk)	
8:22	490	1:3	488
10:7	489	1:4	488
10:14	489	1:5	488
11:2–5	333	1:9	488
11:13	500 n. 10	1:15	488–489
12:28	488–489	6:11	489
15:7	500	8:11–13	489
19:9	134 n. 22	9:1	489
22:40	287	9:2	433 n. 11
23:34–35	287	10:11–12	134 n. 22
24:2–3	492	12:26	271 n. 10

13:2–4	492	21:25–26	492
13:5–8	492	21:27–28	492
13:9–13	492	21:31–32	492
13:14–20	492	24:27	287
13:21–23	492	24:44	287–288, 291,
13:24–25	492		500
13:26–27	492		
13:29–30	492	*John* (Jn)	
13:32	489	1:45	287, 500
			n. 10
Luke (Lk)		3:3	492
1:32	154, 156 n. 17,	3:5	492
	157 n. 20, 330		
1:32–35	157 n. 20	*Acts of the Apostles* (Acts)	
1:33	154, 156 n. 16	1:20	271 n. 10
1:35	154, 330	2:21	508
1:35b	157 n. 20	5:36	326
2	154	13:15	287
3:3	488	13:24	504
3:7	488	21:38	326
3:21	488	26:22	500 n. 10
4:17	271 n. 10	28:23	287
4:18–21	332 n. 26, 333		
7:18–23	333	*Romans* (Rom)	
9:5	489	1:1ff.	244
9:27	489	1:2	272
9:60	490	1:17	500 n. 12
9:62	490	2:24	500 n. 12
10:11	489	3:4	500 n. 12
11:3	489	3:10	500 n. 12
11:20	488–489	3:21	287, 500
11:49–51	287		n. 10
12:16–20	489	4:3	259, 262, 267
12:22–31	489	4:9	259, 262
16:16	287	4:17	500 n. 12
16:18	134 n. 22	4:22	262
16:29	287, 500	6:3–8	815
	n. 10	8:14	815
16:31	287	8:14–17	814
17:20	489	8:36	500 n. 12
17:20–21	489	9:17	500 n. 11
17:23–24	492	9:33	500 n. 12
21:6–7	492	10:11	500 n. 11
21:8–11	492	10:15	500 n. 12
21:12–19	492	12:19	500 n. 13
21:20–24	492	14:11	500 n. 13

1 Corinthians (1 Cor)

1:2	508
1:8	490
1:19	500 n. 13
2:16	490
3:19	500 n. 13
6–7	134 n. 22
7:29	490
15:23	491
15:29	490

2 Corinthians (2 Cor)

10:13	270 n. 4
10:15	270 n. 4
10:16	270 n. 4

Galatians (Gal)

3:6	259, 262, 267
3:10	215 n. 3, 271 n. 10
3:11	244
4:4–7	814 n. 12
4:6	814 n. 14
5:22–23	337
6:16	270, 270 n. 4

Ephesians (Eph)

1:5	814 n. 12
4:2	337

1 Thessalonians (1 Thess)

4:15	490
5:2	490

2 Thessalonians (2 Thess)

2:3–9	491

1 Timothy (1 Tim)

5:18	500 n. 11

2 Timothy (2 Tim)

3:15	272
4:13	271 n. 10

Hebrews (Heb)

4:1–11	41
10:37ff.	244

James (Jas)

2:21	267

2 Peter (2 Pet)

1:14–15	492
3:4	493
3:8–10	493

Jude

14	500
14–15	294

Revelation (Rev) 21, 563

19:11–16	493
19:19–21	494
21	494
21:12	384
21:16	382

(C) Old Testament Apocrypha

Judith (Jdt)

13:6	270 n. 3
16:1	648

Maccabees	499

1 Maccabees (1 Macc)

1:56–57	280
2:50–60	281

2:52	259, 261–262, 267
7:17	281
12:9	272
56–57	280

2 Maccabees (2 Macc)

1:24	530
2:2–3	281

2:13	288, 291	24:10	707 n. 6
2:13–14	281	24–25	642
3:14	530	28–29	636
5:19f.	819	30:15–16	836
10:6–7	361 n. 48	30:18	342 n. 18
15:9	281	34–36	636
		37:11	812 n. 6
4 Maccabees (4 Macc)		38:34–39:1	279
7:21	270 n. 3	42:21	338 n. 10
18:10	283	44:16	308
18:15	288	44:20	259, 262, 267–268
		44–50	308
Sirach (Sir)		46:1	187
1–2	635, 642	47:12	192
4–6	635	49:9	279 n. 24
5:4	337	49:10	308
5:11	337 n. 5	49:14	308
6:15	525	49:15–6	308
6:32	343 n. 21	50:8–9	707 n. 6
7–10	642	50:12	707 n. 6
7–14	636	51:13–30	295
15–26	637		
20	638	*Tobit* (Tob)	
21–22	638	1:4–8	763
23–26	638	13:19	91

(D) OLD TESTAMENT PSEUDEPIGRAPHA

'Aḥiqar		4:6	670
[2:]12	156 n. 18	5:3	671
[4:]55	156 n. 18	6:8	671
		6:9	671
Apocalypse of Abraham (Apoc.Ab.)		7:11	671
17	432	26–30	668
		28:7	668
Assumption of Moses		29:2	668, 670
(As.Mos.)	21	29:4	669
		32:2–4	668
2 Baruch (2 Bar.)	21, 661	32:2–7	671
1:1–3:8	699	32:4	671
1:2	670	35–43	668–669
1:3	670	39:5	669
3:5	670	40:2	668–670
4:3–5	670	40:3	669

53–76	668–669	10:54	666
63:10	661, 669–670	11:1–12:51	665–666
68:5	671	12:33	667
68:6	671	12:34	666–667
70:9	670	12:48	667
71:1	668–670	13:1–58	665, 667
77:8–10	671	13:48	661, 665–667
78:1–87:1	668	13:49	667
79:2	671	14:1–48	665, 667
80:1–2	672	14:18–26	363
85:3	668, 672	14:23–48	282
85:5	672	14:31	667
		14:32	667
1 Enoch (1 En.)	21	14:42–47	363
1:2	295		
1:9	294	*Jubilees* (Jub.)	350, 461
10:1–11:2	295	1:5–18	295
14:1	312	1:12	55 n. 37
46:1–4	154	1:22–28	295
48:1–10	154	1:26–29	295
52:4	154	2:1	295
81:1–2	295	2:2–3	94, 94 n. 29
89	483	3:8–14	295, 299
90	483	3:31	295
93:1	295	6:10	12
		6:11	12
4 Ezra	21, 661	6:17	12
3:1–5:20	665	7:2–4	360
3:2	665	8:22–24	189
3:27	665	8–9	313
4:23	665	10:29–34	189
5:21–6:34	665	13:8–9	360
5:24–25	666, 672	14:6	261
6:19	666	14:10	12
6:35–9:25	665	14:17	12
7:26	666	14:20	12
8:52	666	15:1	12
9:8	666–667	16:29–31	361 n. 48
9:26–10:59	665–667	21:12–14	361
10:7	666	23:11	299
10:20	666	24:22	360
10:27	666	27:1–18	352
10:44	666	27:19–26	360
10:49–50	666	30:1–32:9	315

31:14	11	5:19	91
32:16	781	6:6	91
32:22	781	17	26
33:1–20	390	27	26
34:1–9	431 n. 6	39	26
34:19	39		
44:11	455	*Testament of the Twelve*	
48:12–17	353	*Patriarchs* (T. 12Patr.)	
50:4	181 n. 9	*Testament of Joseph* (T. Jos.)	
50:8	135 n. 25	19:4	329
50:8–13	67	*Testament of Juda* (T. Jud.)	
		3–7	431 n. 6
Liber antiquitatum biblicarum (L.A.B.)		*Testament of Levi* (T. Levi)	
(Pseudo-Philo)	661	2:1	432
7:4	662, 672	2:3	433
10:2	663	2:3–4	431
12:4	663–664	2:4	436
14:2	663	2:5	433–434, 436
19	663	2:5–6	432
19:10	661–663, 672	2:5–4:6	435
19:2	663	2:6	435
19:7	663, 664	2:7–9	434 n. 12
21:6	187	3:1–8	434 n. 12
22:8	195–197, 664	3:4	434
22:8–9	200	3:5	432
22:9	664	4	434
24:3	187	4:2	436
32:3	664	5:1	434–436
65:5	663	5:1–4	391 n. 28
		5:3	435
Psalms of Solomon		5:5	435
(Pss. Sol.)	21	6:1	434
2:37	91	18	329

(E) DEAD SEA SCROLLS AND RELATED TEXTS

I. Cairo Geniza

Aramaic Levi Document (ALD,		2.14–18	436
CLev[Bodl.Cam])	314,	2.16–18	432
	429–437	*3ff.	431
l. 11	432	43.9	191 n. 26
l. 12	432	Bodleian col. a	431
l. 13	432	Cambridge col. b	431

Cairo Damascus
   Document (CD)   33, 290, 349,
                 351, 467,
                 471–472

I, 1	212
I, 3–11	481
I, 4	213
I, 7	800 n. 21
I, 10	54 n. 33
I, 12	467
I, 14	474 n. 30
I, 14–15	471, 473
I, 14–18	467
I, 15	473 n. 27, 474
I, 16	213
I, 18	467
I, 18–19	471
I, 26–27	473 n. 24
II, 1	467, 474
II, 2	212
II, 14	212
II, 14–III, 20	363 n. 54
II, 15	822 n. 37
III, 14	363 n. 51
III, 20–IV, 2	13, 294
IV, 12	255–256
IV, 13–V, 11	467
IV, 15–19	362 n. 50
IV, 19–20	467, 474
IV, 19–V, 1	298
IV, 19–V, 2	133
V, 7–8	467
V, 9–10	132
V, 9–11	132
V, 11–12	472 n. 20
V, 17–19	51
VI, 7	55 n. 35
VI, 13–14	298
VI, 15	100
VI, 19	39
VI, 2	213
VI, 2–11	364
VII, 4–6	146
VII, 4–8	101
VII, 5	132 n. 15

VII, 6–7	100, 131, 146
VII, 15–18	291
VII, 18f.	330
VIII, 12–13	474
IX,4	137 n. 34
IX,5	251
X,6	109
X,7–10	299
X,9–10	299
X,13b	67
X,15	67
XI, 6	40–41
XI, 12	41
XI, 19–21	298
XII, 1–2	135
XII, 22–XIII, 1	36
XII, 23–XIII, 2	329
XIII, 1	100
XIII, 2	109
XIII, 3–4	
XIII, 8	338
XIII, 15–18	100
XIV, 3	100
XIV, 9	101
XIV, 13	100
XIV, 18–19	36
XIV, 18f.	329
XVI, 2–4	294
XVI, 3–4	135 n. 25, 362 n. 50
XIX (ms B)	800 n. 21
XIX,7–9	800 n. 21
XIX,10–11	800 n. 21
XIX,11–12	800 n. 21
XIX,25–26	474
XIX,33–XX,1	254, 329
XX,2	13
XX,5	13
XX,6	55 n. 36
XX,7	13
XX,11	473
XX,11–12	471
XX,13–15	482
XX,14–15	106 n. 36
XX,15	473, 483

A II, 4	343	B XX, 9	342
A VII, 21	345	B XX,14	101
B V, 3–4	343	B XX,32	101

II. Dead Sea Scrolls

1. Index of manuscripts		I, 18	65 n. 16
		I, 20	65 n. 16
Cave 1		I, 24	65 n. 16
1Q3/1QpaleoLev	224	II, 13	448
1Q8/Isaᵇ	152 n. 3,	II, 19	445–446
	460	II, 1a	13
1Q13 10	67	II, 1b	13
1Q14/1QpMic	247, 297	II, 1b–4a	14
4–5	475 n. 32	II, 2	13
8–10	475 n. 32	II, 2b–4a	13
1Q15/1QpZeph	247, 297	II, 21	447
1Q16/1QpPs	297	II, 8	9, 448
1Q20/1QapGen	312	II, 10	65 n. 16
1Q22/1QDM	316	II, 11	65 n. 16
I 1–2	316	II, 11–12	65
1Q23/1QEnGiantsᵃ		II, 3	336
ar	311	II, 8	342
1Q24/1QEnGiantsᵇ?		I–II	000
ar	311	III, 2	444
1Q27/1QMyst	214	III, 3	10
9–10,3	212	III, 5	446
		III, 6	444
1Q28/1QS		III, 7	441, 445
(*Rule of the Community*)	33, 114	III, 8	338
	n. 5, 290,	III, 9	13
	442–443,	III, 18	345
	488	III, 15	445
I, 1–2	54 n. 33	III, 25	447
I, 1–3	290	I–III	451
I, 16	444	I–IV	101
I, 16–III, 6	12	IV	335
I, 21–22a	13	IV, 1	335
I, 22b–24a	13	IV, 2	336
I, 24b–26	13	IV, 3	337, 448
I, 25	444	IV, 4	338, 444
I, 3–5	822 n. 37	IV, 4–6	137 n. 32
I, 7	445	IV, 5	340
I, 16	65 n. 16	IV, 5–6	137

IV, 6	344	VI, 25	9, 448 n. 34
IV, 7	346	VI, 26	445
IV, 11–12	345	VI, 27	444–445
IV, 16	213	VII	103 n. 25,
IV, 18–19	345		107 n. 37,
IV, 20–V, 19	10		451
IV, 24	213	VII, 1	443, 448
IV, 26	444		n. 34
V, 1	104	VII, 2	272, 445
V, 2	13, 102, 444	VII, 3	444
V, 2	485	VII, 4	445
V, 2–3	418 n. 18	VII, 6	443
V, 5–6	9		VII, 6–8
V, 5	340		103
V, 7	105	VII, 7	443
V, 9	13, 55 n. 36,	VII, 8	443
	485	VII, 14	444
V, 9–10	418 n. 18	VII, 16	448 n. 34
V, 10–11	54 n. 33	VII, 17	448 n. 34
V, 11	363 n. 51, 448	VII, 20	443
	n. 34	VII, 21	448 n. 34
V, 12	102	VIII	106, 451
V, 13–14	102	VIII, 1–15	452
V, 14	448	VIII, 2	445
V, 16	443–444	VIII, 3	339
V, 17	272	VIII, 7	299
V, 20	447	VIII, 9	10
V, 26	444, 446	VIII, 10	109
V–VIII	451	VIII, 11	106, 363
V–IX	101		n. 51
VI, 1	251 n. 40, 444	VIII, 11–12	105
VI, 2–3	103	VIII, 12	105
V, 6	55	VIII, 12–16	56 n. 38,
VI, 8–9	137 n. 34		484
VI, 10	105	VIII, 13	97, 445
VI, 11	445	VIII, 13–14	298
VI, 12	105	VIII, 14	272, 441
VI, 14	105	VIII, 15	55 n. 36
VI, 16	105	VIII, 15–IX, 11	451
VI, 17	448 n. 34	VIII, 15b–IX, 11	452
VI, 17–22	102	VIII, 18	9, 13, 339,
V, 19	418 n. 19		448 n. 34
VI, 20	444	VIII, 20	13
VI, 21	448 n. 34	VIII, 21	13, 448, 452
VI, 22	444, 448 n. 34	VIII, 22	448 n. 34

IX, 3–11	452	I, 14	446
IX,6	13	I, 21	8
IX,8	13	I, 21–II, 20	8
IX,9	13	I, 22	443 n. 24
IX,10	452	I, 27	443, 445
IX,11	327, 451	I, 28	446
IX,14	186, 447	I, 28–29	109
IX,16	13	II, 2	109, 446
IX,20–21	485	II, 4	109, 447
IX,24	445	II, 8	446
X,2	444–445	II, 8–9	110
X,3	443	II, 11	110
X,5–6	442	II, 11–22	108, 426 n. 46
X,6	445	II, 12	327
X,9	343, 443	II, 13	446
X,12	445	II, 18ff.	328, 442 n. 19
X,19	444	II, 21	8
X,24	443	II, 21–III, 21	8
X,25	343	II, 22	8, 445
XI, 5	336	III, 1	8
XI, 6	448	III, 2	8
XI, 9	35, 443	III, 22	7
XI, 16	127	III, 22–IV, 19	8
XI, 17	445	IV, 20	7–8
XI, 19	339	IV, 20–V, 19	8
XI, 21	127	IV, 22	8
XXXII, 2	446	V, 20–VI, 20	8
		VI, 1	327
1Q28a/1QSa (*Rule*		XII, 23	327
of the Congregation/		XIV, 19	327
Messianic Rule)	37, 107, 328,	XIV, 20	327
	439, 442–443	XX,1	327
I, 1	7, 445		
I, 1–20	8	1Q28b/1QSb (*Rule*	
I, 2	13, 446	*of Benedictions*)	330, 439, 442
I, 2–3	110	I	442 n. 19
I, 3	109, 446	I, 1	5, 423 n. 37
I, 4	447		448
I, 4–5	139	I, 1–21	3
I, 5–8	448	I, 2	11
I, 6–II, 11	109, 139 n. 39	I, 2–3	9
I, 7	109, 446, 448	I, 3	6–7, 13, 448
	n. 34	I, 19–III	4
I, 10	448	I, 19–III, 19	15
I, 11	138, 445	I, 21	442 n. 19

I, 21–III, 19	3	II, 5–6	19
II, 23	7	II, 6–15	27
II, 24	13	II, 8–9	40
III	4	II, 9–12	19
III, 1	7, 13	II, 13–14	19
III, 21	7, 13	II, 15	27
III, 22	5	II, 15–III, 11	24
III, 22–V, 19	3	II–III, 2	19
III, 22–28	423 n. 38	III, 13	27
III, 23	5, 11	III, 6–7	19
III, 25	7, 11	III, 9–11	19
III, 25–26	14	III, 13–15	19
III, 26	7, 15	III–IV, 2	19
IV, 22	6	IV, 6–7	19
IV, 23	11	IV, 9	27
IV, 24–25	11	V, 3	27
IV, 27	6, 11	V, 16–17	19
IV, 27–28	13	VI, 12	337 n. 5
V, 5	7, 14–15	VII, 3–4	136
V, 20–29	330	VII, 6	136
V, 20	3–6		n. 29
V, 20–VI	3	VII, 3–7, 10–11	19
V, 20–29	423 n. 39	VII–VIII	19
V, 21	6–7, 14–15	VIII, 10	24
V, 23	7	IX,5–9	19
V, 24–25	6	IX,10	27
V, 25	6	IX,17	19
		X,6–8	24
1Q29/1QLit. of Three		X,9–10	19
Tongues of Fire	202 n. 41,	X,13	9
	316	XI, 7	22
1Q32/1QNJ ar	318, 379,	XII, 1	19
	480	XII, 8–16	19
1Q33/1QM		XIII, 8–9	19
(*War Scroll*)	19, 23, 124,	XIII, 9–12	19
	138 n. 35,	XIV, 4–18	19
	152 n. 3,	XV, 2–7	19
	349	XVI, 3	27
I, 1	484 n. 5	XVI, 3–14	19
I, 4–9	19	XVII, 10–14	19
I, 6	25	XIX,1–13	19
I, 11–17	19		
I–II	313, 483	Cave 2	
I–IX	23	2Q13/2QJer	440 n. 12,
II, 1–3	19		699

2Q22/2QapocrDavid?	313–314	4Q53/4QSamᶜ	439,
2Q24/2QNJar	318, 379,		442–443
	381 n. 9,	I	441, 445
	480	I, 5	448
1 3	318	I, 23	443
4 8 7	318	II, 2	444, 448
2Q25/2QJuridical Text	290	II, 24	444
2Q26/2QEnGiants ar	311	III	441, 445
		4Q55/4QIsaᵃ	250
Cave 3		4Q56/4QIsaᵇ	250
3Q4/3QpIsᵃ	297	4Q58/4QIsaᵈ	250
		4Q57/4QIsaᶜ	224, 227
Cave 4		4Q70/4QJerᵃ	92 n. 19,
4Q8/4QGenʰ	114 n. 5		699
4Q9/4QGenʲ	168	4Q71/4QJerᵇ	511, 699
4Q11/4Qpalaeo		4Q72/4QJerᶜ	699
Gen-Exodˡ	165	4Q72a/4QJerᵈ	511, 699
4Q13/4QExodᵇ	534 n. 30	4Q76/4QXIIᵃ	245
4Q22/4QPaleoExodᵐ	219–220,	frg. 1	245
	220 n. 32,	frg. 2–9	245
	227–229,	frg. 7	245
	231, 231	frg. 8–21	245
	n. 84,	frg. 9	245
	232, 461	frg. 10	245
4Q27/4QNumᵇ	219,	frg. 11–18	245
	227–228,	4Q77/4QXIIᵇ	246
	461	4Q78/4QXIIᶜ	246
4Q35/4QDeutʰ	448, 449	4Q79/4QXIIᵈ	
4Q37/4QDeutʲ	228, 229,	1–2	445 n. 32
	232	9	246, 445
4Q38/4QDeutᵏˡ	228–229,		n. 32
	232	4Q80/4QXIIᵉ	247
4Q41/4QDeutⁿ	68,	4Q81/4QXIIᶠ	247
	219–220,	4Q82/4QXIIᵍ	246 n. 20,
	227, 229,		247–248,
	232		251
III, 11	67	frg. 97	248
4Q51/4QSamᵃ	375, 375	frg. 98	248
	n. 35,	frg. 100	248
	599, 599	frg. 101	248
	n. 21,	frg. 102	255–256
	600, 772	4Q119/4QLXXLevᵃ	296
4Q52/4QSamᵇ	152 n. 3,	4Q120/4QpapLXXLevᵇ	296, 507
	767n. 15,	4Q121/4QLXXNum	296
	838	4Q122/4QLXXDeut	296

4Q123/		3–4 II, 8	473 n. 27,
4QpaleoParaJosh	180 n. 7,		475
	317 n. 36	3–4 III, 1a–b	475
4Q128–148 see		3–4 III, 4–5	476 n. 38
4QPhyl		3–4 IV, 5	476 n. 38
4Q149/4QMez A	228–229,	4+3, 1–3	250
	232	4+3, 6–8	250
4Q151/4QMez C	64	4+3, 10ff.	250
4Q156/4QtgLev	296	4Q170/4QpZeph^a	297
4Q157/4QtgJob	296	4Q171/4QpPs^a	472, 473
4Q158	219–220,		n. 24
	229, 231,	4Q172/4QpUnid	121 n. 26,
	231 n. 84,		297, 472,
	232, 237,		473 n. 24
	349,	4Q173/4QpPs^b	297
	351–353,	1	796 n. 11
	450	5	796 n. 11
1, 7–9	351	4Q174/4QFlor	21, 124,
364–367	46		182, 297,
4Q159/4QOrd^a			330
frg. 5	43, 46	frg. 1 2	272
4Q160/4QVisSam	318	frg. 1 12	272
4Q161/4QpIsa^a	138 n. 35	frg. 1 15	272
2, 6–8	472	frg. 1 16	272
8–10	213 n. 21	I 13	195, 201
21–23	213 n. 21		n. 40
4Q162/4QpIsa^b II, 10	472 n. 21	1–2 I, 11	55 n. 35
4Q163/4Qpap pIsa^c		II, 3	294, 498
frg. 1, 4	250, 298		n. 7
4Q164/4QpIsa^d 1 5	195, 201	III, 7	298
	n. 40	4Q175/4QTest	182 n. 13,
4Q165/4QpIsa^e	250		219, 229,
4Q166/4QpHos^a	247, 297		232, 239,
4Q167/4QpHos^b	247, 297		328, 439,
4Q168/4QpMic?	247, 297		442
4Q169/4QpNah	247, 248,	1	441, 447
	297	2	443
2 III, 3	796 n. 11	3	447
2+1, 3f.	250	3–4	448–449
3+4 II, 4–10	250	4	445–446
3+4 III, 3–5	250	5	445
3+4 IV, 3f.	250	5–6	448–449
3–4 I, 1–8	466	7	444–445
3–4 I, 2	466	9	444
3–4 I, 7–8	466	11	445
3–4 II, 1–2	475	14	440 n. 13

14–18	448		4Q213/4QLeviᵃar	
14–20	448		(Aramaic Levi)	212, 436
15	449		6 I–II	212 n. 16
16	447, 449		4Q214/4QLeviᵃ ar	
17	13, 448–449		6 II	212 n. 16
18–19	449		4Q216/4QJubᵃ	
19	441, 449		II, 10–11	94 n. 29
21–30	181, 317		II, 13	55 n. 37
22	445		4Q222/4QJubᵍ	
23	187, 445		1	445
25	448		4	445
28	445		4Q225/4QPsJubᵃ	
4Q176/4QTanḥ	441		2:1, 3–9	265
1–2 I, 6	445		4Q226/4QPsJubᵇ 7:1	267
1–2 I, 10	445		4Q228/4QText with	
4Q177/4QCatena A	297		a Citation of Jubilees	
frg. 2 4	299		frg. 1 I, 1	294
frg. 5–6 11	272		frg. 1 I, 9	294
frg. 7 3	272		4Q232/4QNJ?	480
VIII, 7	472 n. 22		4Q238/4QHab 3	252
IX, 12–13	251		4Q242/4QPrNab ar	153
X, 2–3	251		4Q246/4QapocrDan ar	151, 330
X, 3	251		4Q247/4QPesher on	
frg. 10–11 1	272		the Apocalypse of	
frg. 12–13 I, 2	298		Weeks	297
4Q180/			4Q248/4QHistorical	
4QAgesCreat A	212–213		Text A	441
4Q181/			4Q249/4Qpap cryptA	
4QAgesCreat B	212		Midrash Sefer Moshe	114 n. 5
1 II, 5	213		4Q251/4QHalakhaᵃ A	297, 300
4Q184/4QWiles of			1–2	34
the Wicked			frg. 12	132
Woman	299		4Q252/4QCommGen A	349, 351,
I 2	476 n. 40			363
frg. 1 11–12	299		III, 1–6	363 n. 52
4Q185/4QSapiental			IV, 1–3	808
work	214, 299		IV, 2	796
I, 13	212		V, 2–4	3 n. 1,
I, 13–II, 3	312			330
II, 3	212		4Q253/	
4Q196/			4QCommGen B	349, 351,
4QpapTobᵃ ar	441			363
4Q203/			4Q254/	
4QEnGiantsᵃ ar	311		4QCommGen C	349, 351,
4Q204/4QEnᶜ				363
1 VI, 9	312		4Q256/4QSᵇ	485 n. 7

4Q257/4QpapS^c	114 n. 5, 440	4Q280/4QCurses 1 3	9
2 I, 2	341	4Q284/4QPurification	
4Q258/4QS^d	485 n. 7	Liturgy	136
4Q259/4QS^e	328, 484 n. 6	frg. 2 II	136
		frg. 2 II, 5	136
III, 4	445 n. 34	frg. 3	136
4Q265/4QMiscellaneous		4Q285/4QSerek	
Rules 4Q265	44	ha-Milḥamah	20, 23, 330, 484 n. 5
7, 7	105		
frg. 7 II, 11–17	299	frg. 1	23
4Q266/4QD^a	36	1, 2	7 n. 11
1, 5–6	212	frg. 3	24
3 II, 20–21	100	frg. 4	24
6 II, 2–4	135	frg. 7	25
9 III, 1–7	100	7, 3–4	3 n. 1
9 III, 5	133	7–8	20
10 I, 2	101	frgs. 8–10	26
10 I, 6	100	4Q286/4QBer^a 5 1	10 n. 13
10 I, 12	36 n. 410	4Q287/4QBer^b 2 11	11 n. 17
II	103 n. 25, 107 n. 37	4Q293/4QWork containing Prayers	
11 16b–17	12	C 1 3	7 n. 11
18 V, 4	10	4Q298/4QWords of	
4Q267/4QD^b		the Maskil	212–214
VI, 4–5	134	1–2 i,1–3	212
9 V, 6	101	3–4 ii,3–10	212
9 V, 13	101	3–4 ii,9–10	213
4Q269/4QD^d 8 II, 3–6	35	4Q299/4QMyst^a	
4Q270/4QD^e	331	3a ii,9	212
2 I, 17–18	134	4Q301/4QMyst^c?	
2 II, 15–17	134	5 2	11
2 II, 16	132	5 4	11
2 II, 19–21	212	4Q303/4QMeditation	
2 II, 21	213	on Creation A 1 1	212
7 I, 12–13	134	4Q306/4QMen of	
7 II, 11	12	People who Err 2 3	55 n. 37
4Q271/4QD^f		4Q319/4QOtot 12 2	12 n. 21
2	35	4Q320/4QCalendrical	
3, 9–10	132	Doc A	
3, 12–15	138	4 III, 5	12 n. 21
7 I, 13–15	138	4 IV, 1	12 n. 21
4Q274/4QTohorot A		4 V, 4	12 n. 21
(Purification Rules)	135	4Q321/4QCalendrical	
4Q275/4QCommunal		Doc B	
Ceremony 1 3	12	2 V, 1, 5	12 n. 21

2 VI, 1, 8	12 n. 21	1, 11ff.	314
4Q342/4QLetter? ar	117	1, 12	314
4Q342–348	118	9	213 n. 22
4Q343/4QLetter nab	118	19	314
4Q344/4QDebt		27	213 n. 22
Acknowledgement ar	117	4Q373/	
4Q345/4QDeed A ar		4QapocrJoseph^c 1	116, 313,
or heb 4Q345	118		314
4Q348/4QDeed B		4Q374/4QDiscourse on	
heb? 4Q348	118	the Exodus/Conquest	
4Q350/4QAccount		Tradition	310 n. 17
gr 4Q350	113	9, 3	310 n. 17
4Q351–354	118	4Q375/4QapocrMoses^a	331
4Q356–361	118	4Q375–376	316
4Q359/4QpapDeedC?		4Q376/4QApocryphon	
ar or heb	117	of Moses^a?	124, 331
4Q364/4QRP^b	219,	1 I–II	201 n. 40,
	228–229		202 n. 41
3 II, 1–6	352	4Q377/4QapocrPent.B	
5b II, 13	351 n. 17	2 II, 7	445 n. 29
4Q364–367	349–351,	4Q378/4QapocrJosh^a	179
	353	3 I, 8	318
		11, 1	318
4Q365/4QRP^c		12, 3	318
6a I, 9	353	14	198 n. 38
6a II, 1–7	351	14, 4	318
23	361	22 I, 2–3	198
frg. 23	124	22 II, 7–15	181
23, 10–12	384	4Q378–379	116, 316,
4Q365a/4QT^a?	76, 381,		317 n. 36,
	387, 390,		349
	480		
2	384	4Q379/4QapocrJosh^b	179
2 II	384, 385	1 2	191
	n. 19	3 2	318
		3 4	318
4Q370/4QExhortation		12	181 n. 9
based on the Flood	205, 311,	14 1	318
	349, 351,	17 5	196
	364	22 II	182 n. 13,
1 I 1–3	311, 312		187, 317
1 II, 2	311	22 II, 5	318
1 II, 7	311	22 II, 7	198
I, 3	340	22 II, 9	187
II, 5–7	312	22 II, 12	317
4Q371/4QapocrJoseph^a	116, 313	22 II, 13	116
4Q372/4QapocrJoseph^b	116, 313	22 II, 13–13a	317
1	49		

22 II 14	445	frg. 2 III, 7	808 n. 42
26 2	198	2 III, 17–18	214
4Q381/4QNon-		4Q417 1 I	213
Canonical Psalms		4Q418/4QInstruction^d	
B 24 4–12	86	69 II, 4	213
4Q382/4Qpap		123 4	214
paraKings et al.	300, 440,	184 2	214
	441	4Q419/4QSap. Work B	205 n. 2
1	447	4Q422/4QParaphrase	
2	447	of Gen and Exod	297
4Q385–88	300	4Q424/4QInstruction-	
4Q385a/		like Work	205 n. 2
4QapocrJerC^a 1 II	190	4Q426/4QSapiential-	
4Q385b/4QpsEzek^a	299	Hymnic Work A	212, 214
4Q391/4Qpap psEzek^c	441	1 II, 4	212
4Q394/4QMMT^a		4Q427/4QHod^a	
V, 7–9	361	3	209
4Q394–399/4QMMT	33, 290	3a	209 n. 14
4Q395/4QMMT^b		frg. 7	209 n. 14
29–32	54 n. 31	4Q437/4QBarki	
48–49	132, 135	Napshi^d	117
	n. 26	4Q441/4QIndividual	
59–62	53	Thanksgiving A	439
80–82	133	4Q443/4QPersonal	
4Q396/4QMMT^c 17	498	Prayer	439,
4Q397/4QMMT^d			441–443
C frgs. 14–21,		1	448
lines 14–21	290	1 7	440 n. 13
frg. 18 11	292	2	448
4Q398/4Qpap MMT^c		5	441, 448
11–13 7	55 n. 37	10	448
C frgs. 11–13,		12 I, 3	448
lines 20–21	290	4Q448	205 n. 3
C frgs. 11–17 I, 17–18	290	4Q448A	209
4Q400–407/		4Q451/4QPrayer C	210
4QShirShabb	138 n. 35	4Q457b	440
4Q408/4QapocrMoses^c?	316	I, 7	448
4Q413/4QComp. conc.		II, 6	448
Div. Provid.	205	4Q460/4QNarr. Work	
4Q413a	205	and Prayer	113, 310
4Q415/4QInstruction^a			n. 17
2 II	37	9 I, 3	116, 317
4Q415–418a/		9 I, 5–6	116
4QInstruction	212–213	9 I, 10	119, 122,
4Q416/4QInstruction^b			310 n. 17,
1 13	36		317–318

4Q461/4QNarrative B	310 n. 17	frg. 41, 2	137 n. 31
1 9	310 n. 17	69 2	298
1 10	310 n. 17	4Q513/4QOrdinances[b]	
4Q462/4QNarrative C	441	44	38 n. 8
4Q471/4QWar Scroll-		4Q521/4QMessianic	
like Text B	20	Apocalypse	76, 331,
4Q474/4QText			333
Concerning Rachel		2–4 II, 3	51 n. 22,
and Joseph	310 n. 17		54 n. 33
4	310 n. 17	4Q522/4QProphecy	
5	310 n. 17	of Joshua	316, 317
4Q481/4QapocrElisha	300		n. 36,
4Q491/4Qm[a]	19		769
4Q492/4QM[b]	19	1	198 n. 38
4Q493/4QM[c]	19	5 4	318
4Q494/4QM[d]	19	8	198 n. 38
4Q495/4QM[e]	19	9 I	180, 199
4Q496/4QM[f]	19	9 I 4	192
4Q497/4QpapWar		9 II	179
Scroll-like Text A	19	9 II, 5	318
4Q501/4QapocrLam B	299	9 II, 8	318
4Q502/4QpapRitMar	37, 137,	19 II	192
	440	4Q524/4QT[b]	315–316,
Group I, 2	38 n. 6		380, 441
frg. 2 6	137	4Q525/4QBeat	212
frg. 9 11	137	frg. 1 2	299
frg. 19 2	137	2 II+3,12	212
frg. 19 3	137	2 II+10,3	212
frg. 19 5	137	2 II+13,6	212
frg. 24 4	137	14 II, 15	475 n. 34
frg. 34 3	137	14 II, 18	212
frg. 96 1	137	14 II, 19	212
4Q504/4QDibHam[c]	114 n. 5,	4Q529/4QWords of	
	121 n. 26	Michael ar	20
1–2 III, 12–14	805 n. 34	4Q530–533/4QEn	
4Q508/4QPrFêtes[b]		Giants ar	311
4Q508 2 2–4	39	4Q534/4QNoah[a] ar	330
4Q509/4QpapPrFêtes[c]		4Q539/4QTJoseph	
16 IV, 4	39	ar 4Q539	314
18 1	7 n. 11	2–3 2	212
4Q511/4QShir[b]		4Q541/4QapocrLevi[b]? ar	331
18 II, 8	336	4Q542/4QTQahat ar	212
63 IV, 3	7 n. 11	4Q543/4QVisions of	
4Q512/4QpapRitPur B	136 n. 31	Amram[a] ar 1 1	213, 312
11 4	35	4Q544–549/4QVisions	
36–38 II, 17	35	of Amram	213

4Q545/4QVisions of Amram^c ar 1 I, 1	312	Cave 6	
4Q546/4QVisions of Amram^d ar		6Q8/6QpapEnGiants ar	311
		6Q23/6QWords of Michael?	20
4	212		
14	212	Cave 7	
4Q552/4QFour Kingdoms^a ar	21	7Q1/7QpapLXXExod	296
		7Q2/7QpapEpJer gr	296
4Q553/4QFour Kingdoms^b ar	21	7Q4/7QpapEn gr	296
4Q554/4QNJ^a ar	379, 381, 383	Cave 8	
		8Q3/8QPhyl	62, 65, 228–229, 232
1 I, 5[13]	383		
1 I, 10[18]	383		
1 I, 13[21]	383	12 6	65
1 II	384	15 4	67
1 II, 3[8]	384	8Q4/8QMez	229, 232
1 II, 5[10]	384		
1 II, 12–23	383 n. 15	Cave 11	
XXIII–XXIV	387	11Q5/11QPs^a (Great Psalms Scroll)	124, 294–296, 461, 463, 656
XXXIX,11–XL[1V.]	384		
XL, 14–XLI, 11	384		
XL–XLI	385		
4Q554–555	318, 480		
4Q554a	379, 381	XXVI, 9–15	90
4Q555/4QNJ^b ar	379	XXVI, 13	312
		XXVII, 2–11	294
Cave 5		11Q10/11QtgJob	296
5Q4/5QAmos	247	11Q11/11QapocrPs	205 n. 3
5Q9/5QWork with Place Names	316, 317 n. 36	11Q13/11QMelch	332–333
		II, 18	332
		II, 19	272
1 1	198	11Q14/11QSefer ha-Milḥamah	20
5Q10/5QapocrMal	297	1 II, 13,15	10
5Q15/5QNJ	318, 379, 381, 480	1–2	20
		1–2 II, 4	7 n. 11
1 II, 2	318	11Q18/11QNJ ar	318, 379, 381 n. 9, 480
1 II, 6	318		
II 2–5	318		
5Q16		I, 6–7	318
Frg. 3	796 n. 11	VI, 1	318
		X,5	318
Frg. 5	796 n. 11	11Q19/11QT^a (Temple Scroll)	33, 71,
5Q391	300		

	124,	XXXIX,14–XL[1V.],	
	349–350,	8–9,11,14–XLI, 11	387
	354, 379,	XL, 13ff.	385 n. 19
	381, 384,	XLV, 11–12	135
	388, 390	XLVI, 4	193
I–II	355, 356	XLVII	355
	n. 30	XLVIII, 14–17	135
III, 6	78	XLVIII–LI, 10	355, 356
III–XI	355, 356		n. 30
	n. 30	L, 10–12	136
XII, 8–16	356 n. 30	LI, 4b–10	298
XIII–XXIX	355, 356	LI, 11–66	356 n. 30
	n. 30	LI, 11–LXVI	355
XIV, 2–8	358	LIV, 4	133
XIV, 9–18	359	LVII, 1–5	827
XV, 2–3	358	LVII, 5–11	827
XV, 3–14	362	LVII, 8–9	828
XV, 15–XVII, 5	362	LVII, 11–15	827
XVI	359	LVII, 15–19	827
XVI, 1–3, 8–11	76 n. 12	LVII, 17–18	133
XVII, 10	272 n. 15	LVII, 17–19	133
XVII, 13–14	358	LVII, 19–20	827
XVIII, 2,9 l. 4	359	LVII, 19–21	421
XVIII, 4–7	358	LVII, 20–21	827
XIX, 11–XXIII, 2	360	LVIII, 3–21	827
XX,3–5	358	LVIII, 18	195
XXI, 4–5	361	LVIII, 18–21	203
XXII, 10–11	361	LVIII, 19,21	201 n. 40
XXIII	385 n. 20	LVIII, 20	195
XXIII, 3–XXV, 1	361	LIX,1–21	827
XXIII, 4–5	358	LX,11–18	421
XXIV, 7–8	357	LXIV, 6–13	829
XXV	272	LXIV, 7	830
	n. 15	LXVI, 15–17	132
XXV, 4–6	358		
XXV, 14–15	358, 358	11Q19–20	480
	n. 38	11Q19–21	315
XXVII, 6	67	11Q20/11QT^b	76, 76
XXIX	333		n. 12
XXX	355	2	76 n. 12
XXX, 3–XXXI, 9	316	11Q21/11QT^c?	76
XXX–XLVII	356 n. 30	XQ1–4/XQPhyl 1	238
XXXIV, 12–13	357	2	238
XXXVIII, 13–14	387	3	228–229,
XXXIX,11–13	387		232, 238
		III, 15	60

2. Index of titles

4QAccount gr/4Q350	113
4QAgesCreat A/4Q180	212–213
4QAgesCreat B/4Q181	212
1 II, 5	213
5QAmos 5Q4	247
1QapGen/1Q20	312
4QapocrDan ar/4Q246	151, 330
2QapocrDavid?/2Q22	313–314
4QapocrElisha/4Q481a	300
4QapocrJerCᵃ/4Q385a	
1 II	190
4QapocrJosephᵃ/4Q371	116, 313
4QapocrJosephᵇ/4Q372	116, 313
1	49
1 11ff.	314
1 12	314
9	213 n. 22
19	314
27	213 n. 22
4QapocrJosephᶜ/	
4Q373	116, 313
1	314
4QapocrJoshᵃ/4Q378	116, 179,
	316, 317
	n. 36, 349
3 I, 8	318
11 1	318
12 3	318
14	198 n. 38
14 4	318
22 I, 2–3	198
22 II, 7–15	181
4QapocrJoshᵇ/4Q379	116, 179,
	316, 317
	n. 36, 349
1 2	191
3 2	318
3 4	318
12	181 n. 9
14 1	318
17 5	196
22 II	182 n. 13,
	187, 317
22 II, 5	318

22 II, 7	198
22 II, 9	187
22 II, 12	317
22 II, 13	116
22 II, 13–13a	317
22 II, 14	445
26 2	198
4QapocrLam B/4Q501	299
4QapocrLeviᵇ? ar/	
4Q541	331
4	212
14	212
5QapocrMal/5Q10	297
4QapocrMosesᵃ/4Q375	316, 331
4QapocrMosesᵇ?/4Q376	124, 316,
	331
1 I–II	201 n. 40,
	202 n. 41
4QapocrMosesᶜ?/4Q408	316
4QapocrPent.B/	
4Q377 2 II, 7	445 n. 29
11QapocrPs/11Q11	205 n. 3
1–2 II, 4	7 n. 11
Aramaic Levi see	
4QLeviᵃar	
Aramaic Levi Document	
(ALD, CLevᴮᵒᵈˡ·ᶜᵃᵐ)	314,
	429–437
col. 2, lines 14–18	436
2.16–18	432
*3ff.	431
11	432
12	432
13	432
43.9	191 n. 26
4QBarki Napshiᵈ/	
4Q437	117
4QBeat/4Q525	212
frg. 1 2	299
2 II+3,12	212
2 II+10,3	212
2 II+13,6	212
14 II, 15	475 n. 34
14 II, 19	212
14 II, 18	212

4QBibPar (= 4QRPᵃ)/	
4Q158	219–220,
	229, 231,
	231 n. 84,
	232, 237,
	349,
	351–353,
	450
1, 7–9	351
364–367	46
4QCalendrical	
Doc A/4Q320	
4 III, 5	12 n. 21
4 IV, 1	12 n. 21
4 V, 4	12 n. 21
4QCalendrical	
Doc B/4Q321	
2 V, 1, 5	12 n. 21
2 VI, 1, 8	12 n. 21
4QCatena A/4Q177	297
frg. 2 4	299
frg. 5–6 11	272
frg. 7 3	272
8 7	472 n. 22
9 12–13	251
10 2–3	251
10 3	251
frg. 10–11 1	272
frg. 12–13 I, 2	298
4QCommGen A/4Q252	349, 351,
	363
III, 1–6	363 n. 52
IV, 1–3	808
IV, 2	796
V, 2–4	3 n. 1,
	330
4QCommGen B/	
4Q253	349, 351,
	363
4QCommGen C/	
4Q254	349, 351,
	363
4QCommunal	
Ceremony/	
4Q275 1 3	12

4QComp. conc.	
Div. Provid./4Q413	205
4QCurses/4Q280 1 3	9
frgs. 8–10	26
4QD/4Q266–273	212–213
4QDᵃ/4Q266	36
1 5–6	212
3 II, 20–21	100
6 II, 2–4	135
9 III, 1–7	100
9 III, 5	133
10 I, 2	101
10 I, 6	100
10 I, 12	36 n. 4
10 II	103
	n. 25,
	107 n. 37
11 16b–17	12
18 V, 4	10
4QDᵇ/4Q267	
VI, 4–5	134
9 V, 6	101
9 V, 13	101
4QDᵈ/4Q269	
8 II, 3–6	35
4QDᵉ/4Q270	331
2 I, 17–18	134
2 II, 15–17	134
2 II, 16	132
2 II, 19–21	212
2 II, 21	213
7 I, 12–13	134
7 II, 11	12
4QDᶠ/4Q271	
2	35
3 9–10	132
3 12–15	138
7 I, 13–15	138
4QDebt Acknowl-	
edgement ar/4Q344	117
4QDeed A ar or	
heb/4Q345	118
4QDeed B heb?/	
4Q348	118
4QDeutʰ/4Q35	448, 449

4QDeut^j/4Q37	228, 229, 232	frg. 1 2	272
4QDeut^kl/4Q38	228–229, 232	frg. 1 12	272
		frg. 1 15	272
4QDeut^n/4Q41	68, 219–220, 227, 229, 232	frg. 1 16	272
		1 13	195, 201 n. 40
		1–2 I, 11	55 n. 35
		II, 3	294, 498 n. 7
III, 11	67		
4QDibHam^c/4Q504	114 n. 5, 121 n. 26	III, 7	298
1–2 III, 12–14	805 n. 34	4QFour Kingdoms^a a ar/4Q552	21
4QDiscourse on the Exodus/Conquest Tradition/4Q374	310 n. 17	4QFour Kingdoms^b a ar/4Q553	21
9 3	310 n. 17	4QGen^h/4Q8	114 n. 5
1QDM/1Q22	316	4QGen^j/4Q9	168
I 1–2	316	*Great Psalms Scroll see* 11QPs^a	
4QEn^c/4Q204 1 VI, 9	312	1QH, H^a (*Hodayot*)	124, 212
1QEnGiants^a ar/1Q23	311	II, 30	299
2QEnGiants ar/2Q26	311	IV, 28	7
4QEnGiants^a ar/ 4Q203	311	V, 7	7
		V, 15	9, 345
4QEn Giants^b ar/ 4Q530	311	V, 19	7
		VI, 2	345
4QEn Giants^c ar/ 4Q531	311	VI, 25	9
		VII, 18	9
4QEn Giants^d ar/ 4Q532	311	VII, 21	209
		IX, 8,31	7
4QEn Giants^e ar/ 4Q533	311	IX, 21	339
4QExhortation based on the Flood/ 4Q370	205, 311, 349, 351, 364	IX, 22	35
		IX, 35	340
		IX, 36–37	337
		X, 9	339
		X, 14–15	476
1 I 1–3	311, 312	X, 19	475 n. 34
1 II, 2	311	X, 31–32	476
1 II, 7	311	X, 36	339
I, 3	340	XI, 35–36	345
II, 5–7	312	XII, 5–12	38
4QExod^b/4Q13	534 n. 30	XII, 6–11	476
4QFlor/4Q174	21, 124, 182, 297, 330	XII, 7	473 n. 27
		4QHab 3/4Q238	252
		4QHalakhah^a A/ 4Q251	297, 300

1–2 34
frg. 12 132
4QHistorical Text A/
4Q248 441
4QHod^a/4Q427
3 209
3a 209 n. 14
frg. 7 209 n. 14
1Q*Hodayot* see 1QH, 1QH^a
4QIndividual Thanksgiving
A/4Q441 439
4QInstruction/
4Q415–418a 212–213
4QInstruction^a/4Q415
2 II 37
4QInstruction^b/4Q416
1 13 36
frg. 2 III, 7 808 n. 42
2 III, 17–18 214
4QInstruction^c/
4Q417 1 I 213
4QInstruction^d/4Q418
69 II, 4 213
123 4 214
184 2 214
4QInstruction-like
Work/4Q424 205 n. 2
1QIsa^a 439, 442,
446
n. 37,
447, 450,
732
I 450
I, 1 446
II 450
XXVIII, 18–20 440 n. 12
XXXIII, 7 441,
443–444
XXXV, 15 441
4QIsa$^{a.b.d}$/4Q55, 56, 58 250
1QIsa^b/1Q8 152 n. 3,
460
4QIsa^c/4Q57 224, 227
2QJer/2Q13 440 n. 12,
699

4QJer^a/4Q70 92 n. 19
4QJer^{a,c}/4Q70,72 699
4QJer^{b,d}/4Q71,72a 511, 699
4QJub^a/4Q216
II, 10–11 94 n. 29
II, 13 55 n. 37
4QJub^g/4Q222
1 445
4 445
2QJuridical Text/2Q25 290
4QLetter? ar/4Q342 117
4QLetter nab/4Q343 118
4QLevi^a ar/4Q214
6 II 212 n. 16
1QLit. of three
Tongues of Fire/
1Q29 202 n. 41,
316

4QLXXDeut/4Q122 296
4QLXXLev^a/4Q119 296
4QLXXNum/4Q121 296
1QM (*War Scroll*)/
1Q33 19, 23,
124, 138
n. 35,
152 n. 3,
349
I, 1 484 n. 5
I, 4–9 19
I, 6 25
I, 11–17 19
I–II 313, 483
I–IX 23
II, 1–3 19
II, 5–6 19
II, 6–15 27
II, 8–9 40
II, 9–12 19
II, 13–14 19
II, 15 27
II, 15–III, 11 24
II–III, 2 19
III, 6–7 19
III, 9–11 19
III, 13 27

III, 13–15	19	2–4 II, 3	51 n. 22,
III–IV, 2	19		54 n. 33
IV, 6–7	19	1QMessianic Rule	
IV, 9	27	see 1QSa	
V, 3	27	8QMez/8Q4	229, 232
V, 16–17	19	4QMezuza A/4Q149	228–229,
VI, 12	337 n. 5		232
VII, 3–4	136	4QMezuza C/4Q151	64
VII, 3–7, 10–11	19	4QMiscellaneous	
VII, 6	136 n. 29	Rules/4Q265	44
VII–VIII	19	7 7	105
VIII, 10	24	frg. 7 II, 11–17	299
IX, 5–9	19	4QMMT/4Q394–399	33, 290
IX, 10	27	4QMMTª/4Q394 V,7–9	361
IX, 17	19	4QMMTᵇ/4Q395	
X, 6–8	24	29–32	54 n. 31
X, 9–10	19	48–49	132, 135
X, 13	9		n. 26
XI, 7	22	59–62	53
XII, 1	19	80–82	133
XII, 8–16	19	4QMMTᶜ/4Q396 17	498
XIII, 8–9	19	4QMMTᵈ/4Q397	
XIII, 9–12	19	C frgs. 14–21,	
XIV, 4–18	19	lines 14–21	290
XV, 2–7	19	frg. 18 11	292
XVI, 3	27	1QMyst/1Q27	214
XVI, 3–14	19	9–10,3	212
XVII, 10–14	19	4QMystª/4Q299	
XIX, 1–13	19	3a II, 9	212
4QMª/4Q491	19	4QMystᶜ?/4Q301	
4QMᵇ/4Q492	19	5 2	11
4QMᶜ/4Q493	19	5 4	11
4QMᵈ/4Q494	19	4QNarrative B/4Q461	310 n. 17
4QMᵉ/4Q495	19	1 9	310 n. 17
4QMᶠ/4Q496	19	1 10	310 n. 17
4QMeditation on		4QNarrative C/4Q462	441
Creation A/4Q303		4QNarrative Work	
1 1	212	and Prayer/4Q460	
11QMelch		frg. 9 I, 10	113, 310
11QMelch/11Q13	332–333		n. 17
II, 18	332	9 I, 3	116, 317
II, 19	272	9 I, 5–6	116
4QMen of People		9 I, 10	119, 122,
who Err/4Q306 2 3	55 n. 37		310
4QMessianic			n. 17,
Apocalypse/4Q521	76, 331,		317–318
	333	4QNJ?/4Q232	480

1QNJ ar/1Q32 — 318, 379, 480

2QNJ ar/2Q24 — 318, 379, 381 n. 9, 480

1 3 — 318

4 8 7 — 318

5QNJ ar/5Q15 — 318, 379, 381, 480

1 II, 2 — 318

1 II, 6 — 318

II 2–5 — 318

11QNJ ar/11Q18 — 318, 379, 381 n. 9, 480

I, 6–7 — 318

VI, 1 — 318

X, 5 — 318

4QNJ^a ar/4Q554 — 318, 379, 381, 383, 480

1 I, 5[13] — 383

1 I, 10[18] — 383

1 I, 13[21] — 383

1 II — 384

1 II, 3[8] — 384

1 II, 5[10] — 384

1 II, 12–23 — 383 n. 15

XXIII–XXIV — 387

XXXIX, 11–XL[1V.] — 384

XL, 14–XLI, 11 — 384

XL–XLI — 385

4QNJ^b ar/4Q555 — 318, 379

4QNoah^a ar/4Q534 — 330

4QNon-Canonical Psalms B/4Q381

24 4–12 — 86

4QNum^b/4Q27 — 219, 227–228, 461

4QOrdinances^a/ 4Q159 frg. 5 — 43

4QOrdinances^b/ 4Q513 44 — 38 n. 8

4QOtot/4Q319 12 2 — 12 n. 21

4QpaleoExod^m/4Q22 — 219–220, 220 n. 32,

227–229, 231, 231 n. 84, 232, 461

4QpalaeoGen-Exod^l/ 4Q11 — 165

1QpaleoLev/1Q3 — 224

4QpaleoParaJosh/4Q123 — 180 n. 7, 317 n. 36

4Qpap cryptA Midrash SeferMoshe/4Q249 — 114 n. 5

4Qpap MMT^c/4Q398

11–13 7 — 55 n. 37

C frgs. 11–13, lines 20–21 — 290

C frgs. 11–17 I, 17–18 — 290

4Qpap paraKings et al./4Q382 — 300, 440, 441

1 — 447

2 — 447

4Qpap pIsa^c/4Q163

frg. 1 4 — 250, 298

4Qpap psEzek^c/4Q391 — 441

4QpapDeedC? ar or heb/4Q359 — 117

7QpapEn gr/7Q4 — 296

6QpapEnGiants ar/ 6Q8 — 311

7QpapEpJer/7Q2 gr — 296

7QpapLXXExod/7Q1 — 296

4QpapLXXLev^b/4Q120 — 296, 507

4QpapPrFêtes^c/4Q509

16 IV,4 — 39

18 1 — 7 n. 11

4QpapRitMar/4Q502 — 37, 137, 440

Groupe I, 2 — 38 n. 6

frg. 2 6 — 137

frg. 9 11 — 137

frg. 19 2 — 137

frg. 19 3 — 137

frg. 19 5 — 137

frg. 24 4 — 137

frg. 34 3 — 137

frg. 96 1 — 137

4QpapRitPur B/4Q512	136 n. 31	VII, 10	345
11 4	35	VII, 14	252
36–38 II, 17	35	VIII, 3–13	253
frg. 41, 2	137 n. 31	VIII–XII	465
69 2	298	IX, 2–7	253
4QpapS^c/4Q257	114 n. 5,	IX, 8	10 n. 13
	440	IX, 12–X,5	253
2 I, 2	341	X, 5–13	473
4QpapTob^a ar/4Q196	441	XI, 2–8	255
4QpapWar Scroll-like		XII, 1	10 n. 13
Text A/4Q497	19	XII, 3–4	708 n. 7
4QParaphrase of Gen		XIII, 1	445 n. 32
and Exod/4Q422	297	4QpHos^a/4Q166	247, 297
4QPersonal Prayer/		4QpHos^b/4Q167	247, 297
4Q443	439,	1QPhyl/1Q13 10	67
	441–443	4QPhyl/4Q128–148	
1	448	A	64–65
1 7	440 n. 13	A 2	66
2	448	A 18	64
5	441, 448	B	60,
10	448		64–65,
12 I, 3	448		68
1Q*Pesher Habbakuk* see		B 1	67
1QpHab		B 6	67
4QPesher on the Apocalypse		B 10	61, 62
of Weeks/4Q247	297	B 11–12	59
1QpHab	247, 253,	B 17	62
	297	B 18	65
II, 1–3	472	G	60–61,
II, 1–10	253		63, 66,
II, 6–10	485		228–229,
II, 9–15	253		232
II, 11f.	253	G 5	67
IV, 9–13	254	G 6	61
V	465	G 6–7	61, 63,
V, 8–12	254		68
V, 9–12	472	G 7	61
V, 11–12	472 n. 21	G 7–8	68
VI, 2–5	254	G 10	66
VI, 14	507	G 12–13	60
VI, 16–7:5	273	G 13	60
VII, 2	253	G 18	60
VII, 3–5	486	G 19	67
VII, 5–14	486	G 21–23	68
VII, 7f.	254	G 23–25	60

G 26	63	4QpIsaᵃ/4Q161	138 n. 35
H	65	2, 6–8	472
H 2	64	8–10	213 n. 21
H 3	66, 67	21–23	213 n. 21
	n. 18	4QpIsaᵇ/4Q162	
H 4	62, 66	II, 10	472 n. 21
H 5	62	4QpIsaᵈ/4Q164 1 5	195, 201
H 6	64		n. 40
H 7	59	4QpIsaᵉ/4Q165	250
H 8	62	1QpMic/1Q14	247, 297
H 9	63	4–5	475 n. 32
H 11	65	8–10	475 n. 32
J	64,	4QpMic?/4Q168	247, 297
	228–229,	4QpNah/4Q169	247, 248,
	232		297
J 6	67	2 III, 3	796 n. 11
J 9–10	66	2+1	250
J 15	60	3+4 II, 4–10	250
J 20	67–68	3+4 III, 3–5	250
J 23	63	3+4 IV, 3f.	250
J 24	64	3–4 I, 1–8	466
J 25	61–62	3–4 I, 2	466
J 28	66	3–4 I, 7–8	466
J 37	62	3–4 II, 1–2	475
J 59	65, 67	3–4 II, 8	473 n. 27,
L 12	62		475
M 20–24	65	3–4 III, 1a–b	475
M 24	65	3–4 III, 4–5	476 n. 38
M 26	67	3–4 IV, 5	476 n. 38
O 9–10	68	4+3, 1–3	250
O 21	60	4+3, 6–8	250
8QPhyl/8Q3	62, 65,	4+3, 10ff.	250
	228–229,	1QpPs/1Q16	297
	232	4QpPsᵃ/4Q171	472, 473
12 6	65		n. 24
15 4	67	4QpPsᵇ/4Q173	297
XQPhyl/XQ1–4		4QPrayer C/4Q451	210
1	238	4QPrFêtesᵇ/4Q508	
2	238	2 2–4	39
3	228–229,	4QPrNab ar/4Q242	153
	232, 238	4QProphecy of	
III, 15	60	Joshua/4Q522	316, 317
3QpIsa/3Q4	297		n. 36, 769
2 6–8	472	1	198 n. 38
21–23	213 n. 21	5 4	318

8	198 n. 38	1QRule of the	
9 I	180, 199	Congregation see 1QSa	
9 I 4	192	1QS (Rule of the	
9 II	179	Community)/1Q28	33, 114
9 II, 5	318		n. 5, 290,
9 II, 8	318		442–443,
19 II	192		488
11QPs^a (Great Psalms		I, 1–2	54 n. 33
Scroll)/11Q5	124,	I, 1–3	290
	294–296,	I, 3–5	822 n. 37
	461, 463,	I, 7	445
	656	I, 16	65 n. 16,
XXV, 13	312		444
XXVI, 9–15	90	I, 16–III, 6	12
XXVII, 2–11	294	I, 18	65 n. 16
4QpsEzek^c/4Q385b	299	I, 20	65 n. 16
4QPsJub^a/4Q225 2:1,3–9	265	I, 21–22a	13
4QPsJub^b/4Q226 7:1	267	I, 22b–24a	13
4QpUnid/4Q172	121 n. 26,	I, 24	65 n. 16
	297, 472,	I, 24b–26	13
	473 n. 24	I, 25	444
4QPurification		I–III	451
Liturgy/4Q284	136	I–IV	101
frg. 2 II	136	II, 1a	13
frg. 2 II, 5	136	II, 1b	13
frg. 3	136	II, 1b–4a	14
4QPurification Rules		II, 2	13
see 4QTohorot		II, 2b–4a	13
1QpZeph/1Q15	247, 297	II, 3	336
4QpZeph^a/4Q170	297	II, 8	9, 342,
4QRP^b/4Q364	219,		448
	228–229	II, 10	65 n. 16
3 II, 1–6	352	II, 11	65 n. 16
5b II, 13	351 n. 17	II, 11–12	65
4QRP^c/4Q365		II, 13	448
6a I, 9	353	II, 19	445–446
6a II, 1–7	351	II, 21	447
23	361	III, 2	444
frg. 23	124	III, 3	10
23 10–12	384	III, 5	446
1QRule of Benedictions		III, 6	444
see 1QSb		III, 7	441, 445
1QRule of the		III, 8	338
Community see 1QS		III, 9	13

III, 18	345	V–IX	101
III, 15	445	VI, 1	251 n. 40,
III, 25	447		444
IV	335	VI, 2–3	103
IV, 1	335	VI, 8–9	137 n. 34
IV, 2	336	VI, 10	105
IV, 3	337, 448	VI, 11	445
IV, 4	338, 444	VI, 12	105
IV, 4–6	137 n. 32	VI, 14	105
IV, 5	340	VI, 16	105
IV, 5–6	137	VI, 17	448 n. 34
IV, 6	344	VI, 17–22	102
IV, 7	346	VI, 20	444
IV, 11–12	345	VI, 21	448 n. 34
IV, 16	213	VI, 22	444, 448
IV, 18–19	345		n. 34
IV, 20–V, 19	10	VI, 25	9, 448
IV, 24	213		n. 34
IV, 26	444	VI, 26	445
V, 1	104	VI, 27	444–445
V, 2	13, 102,	VII	103 n. 25,
	444, 485		107 n. 37,
V, 2–3	418		451
	n. 18	VII, 1	443, 448
V, 5	340		n. 34
V, 5–6	9	VII, 2	272, 445
V, 6	55	VII, 3	444
V, 7	105	VII, 4	445
V, 9	13, 55	VII, 6	443
	n. 36,	VII, 6–8	103
	485	VII, 7	443
V, 9–10	418 n. 18	VII, 8	443
V, 10–11	54 n. 33	VII, 14	444
V, 11	363 n. 51,	VII, 16	448 n. 34
	448 n. 34	VII, 17	448 n. 34
V, 12	102	VII, 20	443
V, 13–14	102	VII, 21	448 n. 34
V, 14	448	VIII	106, 451
V, 16	443–444	VIII, 1–15	452
V, 17	272	VIII, 2	445
V, 19	418 n. 19	VIII, 3	339
V, 20	447	VIII, 7	299
V, 26	444, 446	VIII, 9	10
V–VIII	451	VIII, 10	109

VIII, 11	106, 363	XI, 21	127
	n. 51	XXXII, 2	446
VIII, 11–12	105	4QS^b/4Q256	485 n. 7
VIII, 12	105	4QS^d/4Q258	485 n. 7
VIII, 12–16	56 n. 38,	4QS^e/4Q259	328, 484
	484		n. 6
VIII, 13	97, 445	III, 4	445 n. 34
VIII, 13–14	298	1QSa/1Q28a (*Rule*	
VIII, 14	272, 441	*of the Congregation,*	
VIII, 15	55 n. 36	*Messianic Rule*)	37, 107,
VIII, 15–IX, 11	451		328, 439,
VIII, 15b–IX, 11	452		442–443
VIII, 18	9, 13,	I, 1	7, 445
	339, 448	I, 1–20	8
	n. 34	I, 2	13, 446
VIII, 20	13	I, 2–3	110
VIII, 21	13, 448,	I, 3	109, 446
	452	I, 4	447
VIII, 22	448 n. 34	I, 4–5	139
IX, 3–11	452	I, 5–8	448
IX, 6	13	I, 6–II, 11	109, 139
IX, 8	13		n. 39
IX, 9	13	I, 7	109, 446,
IX, 10	452		448 n. 34
IX, 11	327, 451	I, 10	448
IX, 14	186, 447	I, 11	138, 445
IX, 16	13	I, 14	446
IX, 20–21	485	I, 21	8
IX, 24	445	I, 21–II, 20	8
X, 2	444–445	I, 22	443 n. 24
X, 3	443	I, 27	443, 445
X, 5–6	442	I, 28	446
X, 6	445	I, 28–29	109
X, 9	343, 443	II, 2	109, 446
X, 12	445	II, 4	109, 447
X, 19	444	II, 8	446
X, 24	443	II, 8–9	110
X, 25	343	II, 11	110
XI, 5	336	II, 11–22	108, 426
XI, 6	448		n. 46
XI, 9	35, 443	II, 12	327
XI, 16	127	II, 13	446
XI, 17	445	II, 18ff.	328, 442
XI, 19	339		n. 19

II, 21	8	IV, 22	6
II, 21–III, 21	8	IV, 23	11
II, 22	8, 445	IV, 24–25	11
III, 1	8	IV, 27	6, 11
III, 2	8	IV, 27–28	13
III, 22	7	V, 5	7, 14–15
III, 22–IV, 19	8	V, 20	3–6
IV, 20	7–8	V, 20–29	330, 423
IV, 20–V, 19	8		n. 39
IV, 22	8	V, 20–VI	3
V, 20–VI, 20	8	V, 21	6–7,
VI, 1	327		14–15
XII, 23	327	V, 23	7
XIV, 19	327	V, 24–25	6
XIV, 20	327	V, 25	6
XX, 1	327	4QSam^a/4Q51	375, 375
1QSb (*Rule of*			n. 35,
Benedictions)/1Q28b	330, 439,		599, 599
	442		n. 21,
I	442 n. 19		600, 772
I, 1	5, 423	4QSam^b/4Q52	152 n. 3,
	n. 37,		767 n. 15,
	448		838
I, 1–21	3	4QSam^c/4Q53	439,
I, 2	11		442–443
I, 2–3	9	I	441, 445
I, 3	6–7, 13,	I, 5	448
	448	I, 23	443
I, 19–III	4	II, 2	444, 448
I, 19–III, 19	15	II, 24	444
I, 21	442 n. 19	III	441, 445
I, 21–III, 19	3	4QSapiential Work/	
II, 23	7	4Q185	214, 299
II, 24	13	I, 13	212
III	4	I, 13–II, 3	312
III, 1	7, 13	II, 3	212
III, 21	7, 13	4QSapiential Work	
III, 22	5	A/4Q426	212, 214
III, 22–28	423 n. 38	1 II, 4	212
III, 22–V, 19	3	4Q448	205 n. 3
III, 23	5, 11	4Q448A	209
III, 25	7, 11	4Q457b	440
III, 25–26	14	I, 7	448
III, 26	7, 15	II, 6	448

4QSapiential Work
  B/4Q419   205 n. 2
11QSefer
  ha-Milḥamah/
  11Q14   20
  1 II, 13,15   10
  1–2   20
4QSerek
  ha-Milḥamah/
  4Q285   20, 23,
      330, 484
      n. 5
  frg. 1   23
  1 2   7 n. 11
  frg. 3   24
  frg. 4   24
  frg. 7   25
  7 3–4   3 n. 1
  7–8   20
4QShir[b]/4Q511
  18 II, 8   336
  63 IV, 3   7 n. 11
4QShirShabb/
  4Q400–407   138 n. 35

11QT[a]
  (Temple Scroll)/11Q19   33, 71,
      124, 315,
      349–350,
      354, 379,
      381, 384,
      388, 390,
      480
  I–II   355, 356
      n. 30
  III, 6   78
  III–XI   355, 356
      n. 30
  XII, 8–16   356 n. 30
  XIII–XXIX   355, 356
      n. 30
  XIV, 2–8   358
  XIV, 9–18   359
  XV, 15–XVII, 5   362
  XV, 2–3   358

XV, 3–14   362
XVI   359
XVI, 1–3, 8–11   76 n. 12
XVII, 10   272 n. 15
XVII, 13–14   358
XVIII, 4–7   358
XIX, 11–XXIII, 2   360
XX, 3–5   358
XXI, 4–5   361
XXII, 10–11   361
XXIII   385 n. 20
XXIII, 3–XXV, 1   361
XXIII, 4–5   358
XXIV, 7–8   357
XXV   272 n. 15
XXV, 4–6   358
XXV, 14–15   358, 358
    n. 38
XXVII, 6   67
XVIII, 2,9 l. 4   359
XXIX   333
XXX   355
XXX, 3–XXXI, 9   316
XXXIV, 12–13   357
XXX–XLVII   356 n. 30
XXXVIII, 13–14   387
XXXIX, 11–13   387
XXXIX, 14–XL[1V.],
    8–9,11,14–XLI, 11   387
XL, 13ff.   385 n. 19
XLV, 11–12   135
XLVI, 4   193
XLVII   355
XLVIII, 14–17   135
XLVIII–LI, 10   355, 356
    n. 30
L, 10–12   136
LI, 4b–10   298
LI, 11–66   356 n. 30
LI, 11–LXVI   355
LIV, 4   133
LVII, 5–11   827
LVII, 8–9   828
LVII, 11–15   827
LVII, 15–19   827

LVII, 17–18	133	7	444–445
LVII, 17–19	133	9	444
LVII, 1–5	827	11	445
LVII, 19–20	827	14	440 n. 13
LVII, 19–21	421	14–18	448
LVII, 20–21	827	14–20	448
LVIII, 3–21	827	15	449
LVIII, 18	195	16	447, 449
LVIII, 18–21	203	17	13, 448–449
LVIII, 19,21	201 n. 40	18–19	449
LVIII, 20	195	19	441, 449
LIX, 1–21	827	21–30	181, 317
LX, 11–18	421	22	445
LXIV, 6–13	829	23	187, 445
LXIV, 7	830	25	448
LXVI, 15–17	132	28	445
4QTᵃ?/4Q365a	76, 381, 387, 390, 480	4QText Concerning Rachel and Joseph/4Q474	310 n. 17
4QTᵇ/4Q524	315–316, 380, 441	4	310 n. 17
		5	310 n. 17
11QTᵇ/11Q20	76, 76 n. 12, 315, 480	4QText with a Citation of Jubilees/4Q228	
		frg. 1 I, 1	294
col. 2	76 n. 12	frg. 1 I, 9	294
11QTᶜ?/11Q21	76, 315	4QtgJob/4Q157	296
4QTanḥ/4Q176	441	11QtgJob/11Q10	296
1–2 I, 6	445	4QtgLev/4Q156	296
1–2 I, 10	445	4QTJoseph ar/4Q539	314
4QTempleᵃ see 4QTᵃ?		2	384
4QTempleᵇ see 4QTᵇ		2–3 2	212
11QTemple Scroll see 11QTᵃ		2 II	384, 385 n. 19
4QTest/4Q175	182 n. 13, 219, 229, 232, 239, 328, 439, 442	4QTohorot A (Purification Rules)/ 4Q274	135
		4QTQahat ar/4Q542	212
		4QVisions of Amram/ 4Q544–549	213
1	441, 447	4QVisions of Amramᵃ ar/4Q543 1 1	312
2	443		
3	447	4QVisions of Amramᶜ ar/4Q545 1 I, 1	312
3–4	448–449		
4	445–446	4QVisions of Amramᵈ ar/4Q546	
5	445		
5–6	448–449		

4QVisSam/4Q160	318	4QXII^a/4Q76	245
4QWar Scroll-like		frg. 1	245
Text B/4Q471	20	frg. 2–9	245
4QWiles of the Wicked		frg. 7	245
Woman/4Q184	299	frg. 8–21	245
1 2	476	frg. 9	245
	n. 40	frg. 10	245
frg. 1 11–12	299	frg. 11–18	245
4QWords of the		4QXII^b/4Q77	246
Maskil/4Q298	212–214	4QXII^c/4Q78	246
1–2 i,1–3	212	4QXII^d/4Q79	
3–4 ii,3–10	212	1–2	445 n. 32
3–4 ii,9–10	213	9	246, 445
6QWords of Michael?/			n. 32
6Q23	20	4QXII^e/4Q80	247
4QWords of Michael		4QXII^f/4Q81	247
ar/4Q529	20	4QXII^g/4Q82	246 n. 20,
4QWork containing			247–248,
Prayers C/			251
4Q293 1 3	7 n. 11	frg. 97	248
5QWork with Place		frg. 98	248
Names/5Q9	316, 317	frg. 100	248
	n. 36	frg. 101	248
1 1	198	frg. 102	255–256

III. Wadi Muraba'at (Mur)

42	121	89–107	116 n. 9
47	121	Greek scroll of the	
88	244, 246	Twelve Prophets	507
	n. 20, 256		

IV. Naḥal Ḥever

P. Ḥever 7	117	8Hev	
32	117	XII gr	243, 246
			n. 20,
			252, 256

V. Naḥal Mishmar

1Mish 2, 34Se 5	117 n. 9

VI. Masada

Mas1/MasGen	454		316, 317
Mas1a/MasLev^a	458		n. 36
Mas1k/MasShirShabb		Mas 1n	120 n. 24
i 6	120		
Mas 1l/MasapocrJosh	180 n. 7,	PAM 43.676 45 2	7 n. 11

(F) PHILO

De vita contemplativa 25	283	*De praemiis et poenis*	
Quis rerum divinarum		165ff.	325, 325
heres 19 §94–95	262		n. 9
Legum allegoriae 3.81 §228	262		
De vita Mosis 2.25–44	502 n. 16	*Quod omnis probus*	
De mutatione nominum		*liber sit* (*Prob.*) 87	137 n. 34
33 §177	262	*De virtutibus* (*Virt.*) §70	203 n. 43

(G) JOSEPHUS

Josephus	325	XII, §323	648
		XIII, §296	469
Contra Apionem/Against		XIII, §297	469
Apion (*Ap.*)		XIII, §301	483 n. 4
1 §§37–42	284	XIII, §372–383	249
		XIII, §376–418	466
Antiquitates Judaicae/		XIII, §380ff.	250
Jewish Antiquities (*Ant.*)		XIV, §105–109	253
I, 10, 3 §183	262	XVIII, §85	326
I, §70	480	XVIII, §288–296	416 n. 11
III, §214–215	201 n. 40	XX, §97	326
III, §217	203 n. 42	XX, §97–99	492
III, §218	202 n. 41	XX, §169–172	326, 492
III, §250	359 n. 41		
IV, §165	187, 203	*Bellum Judaicum* (*B.J.*)/	
	n. 43	*Jewish War* (*J.W.*)	
V, §20	187	I, §70	483 n. 4
V, §55	194 n. 32	I, §88–98	249
V, §59	193 n. 30	I, §92–114	466
V, §68	197	II, 17,6, §425	361
VI, §214	648	II, §129	35
VII, §80	648	II, §146	137 n. 34
IX, §35	648	II, §161	35

II, §261–263	492	VII, §437ff.	326
IV, §§334–44	287	X, §35	284
VII, §29	326		

(H) Rabbinical and Medieval Jewish Literature

I. Mishna

m. ’Avot 1:1	468 n. 6	7:8	827
m. Ber. 2:2	487	9	202 n. 41
m. Bik. 1:4	817 n. 19	12	202 n. 41
m. Ḥul. 4:3	136 n. 30	m. Taʿan.	
m. Menaḥ.		4:5	361
9:4	357	4:8	38
9:6	358	m. Yad. 4:6	272
m. Peʾah		m. Yoma 7:4	38
5:6	842	m. Zebaḥ.	
7:3	842	14	768
m. Šabb. 2:2	805 n. 32	14:4–6	197, 200
m. Soṭah		14:4–8	765
2:1	359 n. 41		

II. Tosefta

t. Bik. 1:2	823 n. 43, 824	13	200
	n. 46	14	200
t. Zebaḥ.			
6	200		

III. Talmud Bavli

b. B. Bat.		b. Ketub.	
14b	296, 807	1, 25c	367 n. 1
	n. 36	65b	367 n. 1
15a	296	b. Meg.	
60b	821 n. 36	18b	59 n. 11
122a	200	29a	818 n. 25, 819
b. B. Qam. 7a	231		n. 29
b. Ber.		b. Menaḥ.	
8a	354 n. 27	53b	191 n. 27
58a	367 n. 1	68b	359 n. 41
b. Giṭ.		b. Pesaḥ. 68b	12
56:2	710 n. 18	b. Qidd.	
76b	367 n. 1	2b	37

29b	132 n. 16	*b. Sukkah* 29a	371
66a	416 n. 10	*b. Šebu.* 88a	12
b. Roš Haš. 27a	229	*b. Taʿan.*	
b. Šabb. 28:9–10	748	7a	37
28:11–15	748	28a	361
b. Sanh.		30b	821 n. 36
16a	203 n. 42, 204	*b. Tem.*	
	n. 44	28b–29a	766 n. 13
49a	203 n. 43	30b	367 n. 1
94a	823 n. 43	*b. Yebam.*	
b. Soṭah		46a–47b	816 n. 17
1	367 n. 1	79a	377
2	367 n. 1	*b. Yoma*	
11a	371	12a	193 n. 29
16c	367 n. 1	21:2	710 n. 18
33b	215 n. 1, 780	39:2	710 nn. 18–19
	n. 41	73b	203 n. 43,
37a	193 n. 29		204 n. 44
48b	202 n. 41,	*b. Zebaḥ* 118b	193 n. 29,
	800 n. 21		200

IV. Talmud Yerushalmi

y. Ber. 4:2	822 n. 39	*Y. Sanh.* 2:20c	377
y. Bik. 1:4	823 n. 43, 824	*y. Soṭa*	
	n. 46	7:3	780 n. 41
y. Meg. 1:12	193 n. 29	7:3 (21c)	215 n. 1
Y. Moʾed Qaṭ.		*y. Taʿan.* 68d	487
1:80d	367 n. 1	*y. Yoma*	
y. Peʾah		4:1	200
8:21	367 n. 1	4:4	710 n. 18
19a	842	6:3	710 n. 18
y. Pesaḥ. 6:1 (33a)	217 n. 17	10:1	200
y. Qidd. 4:1	194 n. 33, 202		
	n. 41		

V. Targumim

Aramaic Targum	231 n. 86	*Tg. Pseudo-Jonathan*	
Tg. Onqelos		(*Tg. Ps.-J.*)	187, 263
(*Tg. Onq.*)	187, 192, 263	1	263
Tg. Neofiti		*Tg. Jonatan*	244
(*Tg. Neof.*)	231		

VI. Midrashim and other rabbinic and medieval Jewish texts

'Abot de Rabbi Nathan ('Abot R. Nat.)
   Version A, 4   710 n. 18
   Version B, 7   710 n. 18
   Version B, 25   710 n. 18,
                  710 n. 19

Gen Rabbah
   15:2   710 n. 18
   55:7   714

Exod Rabbah
   1:32   823 n. 43
   2:5   820 n. 33
   17:2   711 n. 21
   23:5   710 n. 17,
                  711 nn.
                  20–21,
                  714 n. 32
   30:24   819 n. 28
   35:1   710 n. 18

Lam. Rab. 1:13 [41]   487

Lev Rabbah
   1:2   710 n. 18,
                  710 n. 19,
                  711 n. 20
   1:4   676 n. 5
   6–7   676 n. 5
   16   676
   17:10–11   675 n. 3
   17:11   676, 676
                  n. 5
   25:1   371
   34:13   367 n. 1

Maimonides
   b. Yeb. 22a   817 n. 19
   b. Yeb. 48b   817 n. 19
   Gerim 1:1–5   816 n. 17
   Hagahot Maimuniot 15 176 n. 27
   Hilkhot 'Issurei Bi'ah
      14:1–5   816 n. 17

Hilkhot Kelei Mikdash
   6.5   361
Letter to Obadiah the
   Proselyte   817 n. 19

Mekilta: see Mek. de
   Rabbi Yishmael

Mek. de Rabbi Simon
   Bar Johai 17:14   710 n. 18

Mek. de Rabbi Yishmael 230, 367
                      n. 2,
                      371
   Amalek, ch. 2   710 n. 18,
                      819 n. 26
   Beshalah   187, 352,
                      710 n. 18
   Mishpatim   230
   Pisha, ch. 14   818 n. 25
   Shirta 6   814 n. 11

Midrash Tannaim
   Deut 1:7   711 n. 21

Midrash Tanhuma   367 n. 2

Midrash Tehillim 91 819 n. 2

Midrash wayyisa'u   431 n. 6

Num Rabbah
   8:1   710 n. 18
   8:4   194 n. 33
   12:4   710 n. 18
   12:9   187

Pesharim   351

Pesher Habakkuk   252, 472
   2:8   422
                  n. 34

Pesher Joshua
6 — 239
26 — 239

R. Akiva 4:12 — 749 n. 37

Rashi
  Num 23:9 — 820 n. 31
  Exod 15:21 — 352

Seder Olam Rabbah
  11 — 197, 200
  30 — 482

Sekhel Tov 2.324–325 — 819 n. 26

Shulhan Arukh
  Even HaEzer, 129:20 — 817 n. 20
  Yoreh Deah 268:2 — 816 n. 17

Sifra, Numbers 84 — 367 n. 2

Sifre Deut./Sifre Devarim
  6 — 710 nn. 18–19, 711 n. 21
  11:30 — 215 n. 1
  28 — 710 n. 18
  56 — 780 n. 41
  153 — 420 n. 26
  175:70 — 766 n. 14
  352 — 191 n. 27, 193

Sifre Num.
  sec. 78 — 823 n. 43
  sec. 81 — 824 n. 46
  84 — 814 n. 11, 818 n. 25

134 — 710 n. 18

Sopherim 2:4 — 176 nn. 26, 28

Song of Songs Rabbah/ Song Rabba — 710 n. 17
  3:3 — 710 n. 18
  4:2 — 711 n. 21

Song of songs Zuta/ Song Zuta — 710 n. 17
  1:1 — 711 n. 21
  4:8 — 710 n. 18, 714 n. 32

Tanhuma
  Beshallah sec. 28 — 819 n. 26
  Lekh Lekha 6 — 817 n. 19

Tanh. Buber
  Balak, 19 — 820 n. 31
  Lekh Lekha 6 — 817 n. 19
  Yitro 5 — 823 n. 43
  7 — 823 n. 43

Yalqut: see *Yalqut Shimeoni*

Yalqut Shimeoni — 367 n. 2
  Vayishlah, §132 — 352
  1.267 — 819 n. 26
  2.82 — 819 nn. 26, 28
  2.92 — 818 n. 25, 819 n. 29
  2.577 — 819 n. 28
  sec. 726 — 824 n. 45
  268 — 823 n. 43

(I) Classical and Ancient Christian Writings

Aeschines 2.22   519 n. 16

Aristeas, Letter to (Arist.)
  312–317   502 n. 15

Aristophanes, Scholion to
  (1263bis 1)   652

Clement of Alexandria
Stromateis
  I, 23,154,2f.   307
  I, 141,1–2   306
  I, 141,2   483 n. 4

1 Clement (1 Clem.)
  7:2   270 n. 5
  53:1   272

Diodorus Siculus, *Bibliotheca*
  1,70   828 n. 5
  1,70,91   828

Euchologium   563

Eusebius
Historia Ecclesiastica
  (3.25; 6.25)   269
Praeparatio Evangelica
  IX,15   306
  IX,16   306
  IX,18   307
  IX,19.4   306
  IX,21,1–19   306
  IX,22,1   309
  IX,22,2   309
  IX,22,3   309
  IX,22,4–6   309
  IX,22,7   309
  IX,22,8–9a   309
  IX,22,9b   309
  IX,22,10–1   309
  IX,23   307
  IX,24   272
  IX,27   307

  IX,27.7   308
  IX,29.1–3   306

Herodotus (Hdt.)
  I 23   530 n. 20
  I 25   530 n. 20
  I 26   530 n. 20

Irenaeus
Adversus haereses
  1.9.4–5   270 n. 5
  3.2.1   270 n. 5
  3.11.1   270 n. 5

Origen, *Hexapla* 6.16   113 n. 1

Plato
Protagoras (Prot.)
  310 A   530 n. 20
  310 B   530 n. 20
  315 B   530 n. 20
  315 C   530 n. 20

Plautus
Amphitryon 960f.   812 n. 7
Menaechmi 110f.   812 n. 8

Sibylline Oracles   21
  110–61   313

Tacitus, *Historiae*
  V, 13.2   326

Thucydides (Thuc.)
  I, 108,2   532 n. 26
  I, 126,2   532 n. 26

Xenophon Atheniensis,
  Anabasis 4.2.25–28   649

Xenophon Ephesius
Ephesiaca A
  I 3,4   530 n. 20
  II 2   530 n. 20

(J) PAPYRI

PAmherst		Pcorn	519 n. 15
003(c1)	551	P. Eleph. 1, ll. 4–13	537 n. 39
003(c2)	551	P. Fuad 266	261 n. 6
004	551	PHib 1	519 n. 15
005	551	2	519 n. 15
006	552	PLille 1	519 n. 15
007	551	2	519 n. 15
191(a)	551	PMich 1	519 n. 15
191(b)	552	3.174	653
192	551	P. Nash	228–229,
193	552		232
194(a)	552	104, ll. 13	537 n. 39
198	552	104, ll. 16	537 n. 39
200	552	104, ll. 23	537 n. 39
PCairZen 1.59057.1–4	521	104, ll. 27	537 n. 39
1–5	519 n. 15	104, ll. 30	537 n. 39
2.59155.1–3	520	104, ll. 32	537 n. 39
5.59816.1–4	521	POslo 3.27	653
5.59852.7–10	521	POxy 50.3555	653
P. Chester Beatty,		PPetr 1–3	519 n. 15
Manichaean Psalm Book	563	PSI 4	519 n. 15
PCol 3	519 n. 15	4.420.1–19	522
4	519 n. 15	5	519 n. 15
4.66.1–9	522	6	519 n. 15

(K) NEAR EASTERN TEXTS

ARM (Archives royales de Mari) 8:1	811	*CAD* (*The Assyrian Dictionary of the Oriental Institute of the University of Chicago*)	
BGU (*Ägyptische Urkunden aus den Königlichen Staatlichen Museen zu Berlin, Griechische Urkunden*)		A 1.97–98	756 n. 9
		A 2.279	755 n. 6
		D 61bc–62a	
		E 69	756 n. 9
4. 1139	653	L 116d	812 n. 6
4. 1182	653	M 1.180	755 n. 2
4. 1200	653	M 186	755 n. 2
11052, ll. 22	537 n. 39	N 1.204–206	755 n. 4
		S 9	755 n. 4
11052, ll. 7	537 n. 39	S 68–69	755 n. 4
		S 74	755 n. 4
		Ṣ 137a–138b	812 n. 6

INDEX OF NAMES

Abegg, M. G.   3 n. 5, 208 n. 10, 265 n. 20, 266 n. 23, 273 n. 16, 328 n. 18, 336 n. 1, 448 n. 44, 592 n. 4

Abel, F. M.   223 n. 48

Abusch, T.   683 n. 27

Aejmelaeus, A.   525 n. 1, 526 n. 3

Aharoni, Y.   836 n. 5

Ahrend, M. A.   714 n. 34

Albani, M.   313 n. 23

Albeck, H.   842 n. 29

Albrektson, B.   498 n. 5, 776 n. 35

Albright, W. F.   228 n. 75, 795 n. 4

Alexander, P. S.   23 n. 5, 108 n. 45, 149 n. 81, 328 n. 17, 354 n. 24, 443 n. 27

Allegro, J. A.   43 n. 2, 181 n. 10, 219 n. 26, 248 n. 35, 439 n. 3, 466 n. 2

Allen, L. C.   621 n. 7, 621 n. 9

Allen, W. H.   128 n. 4

Alliata, E.   314 n. 30

Alon, G.   223 n. 50

Altheim, F.   313 n. 25

Altmann, A.   52 n. 26

Aly, Z.   261 n. 6

Anbar, M.   778 n. 36

Anderson, A. A.   248 n. 35

Anderson, F. I.   700 n. 3

Anderson, G. A.   358 n. 37

Anderson, R. T.   215 n. 5

Anz, H.   524

Arndt, W. F.   647

Astren, F.   114 n. 4

Attridge, H. W.   91 n. 17, 265 n. 21, 431 n. 5, 605 n. 1, 797 n. 11

Auld, A. G.   58 n. 6

Austermann, F.   505 n. 23

Avalle, D'A. S.   761 n. 6

Avemarie, F.   102 n. 22

Avery-Peck, A. J.   110 n. 51

Avigad, N.   224 n. 54

Avishur, Y.   843 n. 31

Bacher, W.   708 n. 8

Bacon, B. W.   778 n. 36

Baillet, M.   19 n. 2, 137 n. 32, 180 n. 6, 220 n. 32, 228 n. 76

Ball, C. J.   792 n. 67

Ballard, M.   643 n. 15

Bandstra, B. L.   529 n. 16

Bardtke, H.   98 n. 9

Barnes, W. E.   368 n. 2

Bar-On, S.   745 n. 13

Barr, J.   647

Barrera J. T.   97 n. 3, 128 n. 5, 129 n. 8, 279 n. 21, 295 n. 54, 347 n. 4, 351 n. 13, 457 n. 9, 460 n. 16, 499 n. 8

Barth, L. M.   804 n. 31

Barthélemy, D.   138 n. 36, 224 n. 56, 405 n. 24, 621 n. 7, 733 n. 7

Barthélemy, J. D.   369 n. 11, 408 n. 32

Barthélemy, O. P.   3 n. 2

Barton, J.   286 n. 35

Barzilai, G.   363 n. 52

Baumgarten, A.   100 n. 14, 466 n. 4, 470 n. 15

Baumgarten, J. M.   36 n. 5, 44, 44 n. 4, 101 n. 18, 104 n. 28, 105 n. 31, 134 n. 24, 137 n. 33, 138 n. 36, 146 n. 70, 331 n. 22, 419 n. 24, 420 n. 28, 469 n. 12

Baumgartner   79 n. 22

Beall, T. S.   98 n. 7, 144 n. 63
Beck, C. H.   305 n. 3
Beckman, G.   829 n. 8
Beckwith, R. T.   272 n. 14, 285 n. 31
Behrens, A.   258 n. 4
Bengtsson, H.   466 n. 4
Ben-Hayyim, Z.   160 n. 6, 216 n. 11
Benoit, P.   116 n. 9, 244 n. 13
Ben-Porat, Z.   95 n. 31
Bergren, T. A.   597 n. 16
Berlin, A.   85 n. 5
Bernstein, B.   642 n. 13
Bernstein, M. J.   49 n. 19, 119 n. 20, 149 n. 81, 347 n. 1, 363 n. 52, 796 n. 9
Bertram, G.   505 n. 24
Beuken, W. A. M.   736 n. 16
Beyer, H. W.   269 n. 1
Beyer, K.   384 n. 16, 392 n. 30
Beyerle   246 n. 22
Biesenthal, H. R.   757 n. 19
Black, M.   367 n. 2
Blass   261 n. 7
Bloch, R.   409 n. 35
Block, D. I.   621 n. 7
Blum, E.   792 n. 68, 804 n. 30
Boccaccini, G.   106 n. 36
Bock, H. N.   792 n. 69
Bodine, W. R.   526 n. 4, 528 n. 11, 564 n. 7
Boer, M. C. de   151 n. 2
Bogaert, P.-M.   664 n. 4
Böhl, F. M. T.   374 n. 30
Borger, R.   734 n. 9, 756 n. 8
Born, A. van den   621 n. 8
Boshnino, A.   226 n. 65
Bouche-Leclerq, A.   726 n. 12
Bowden, J. S.   369 n. 10
Bowker, J.   263 n. 13
Boyer, G.   811 nn. 1, 4
Brann, M.   833 n. 1
Braun, O.   114 n. 2

Brenton, C. L.   574 n. 7
Brettler, M.   475 n. 33, 755 n. 4
Breytenbach, C.   333 n. 29
Briggs, C. A.   647
Briggs, E. G.   647
Bright, J.   92 n. 19
Brin, G.   135 n. 25, 350 n. 11, 829 n. 6, 831 n. 19
Brock, S. P.   114 n. 2, 539 n. 9, 643 n. 15, 733 n. 6
Brockelmann, C.   505 n. 21
Brook, A. E.   372 n. 25
Brooke, A. E.   563 n. 5, 571 n. 2
Brooke, G. J.   52 n. 26, 58 n. 6, 63 n. 13, 66 n. 17, 79 n. 24, 105 n. 33, 138 n. 35, 347 n. 1, 349 n. 7, 362 n. 49, 363 n. 52, 380 n. 6, 424 n. 43, 439 n. 5, 796 n. 7
Brooten, B.   129 n. 10
Broshi, M.   72 n. 7, 97 n. 1, 117 n. 10, 128 n. 6, 201 n. 40, 316 n. 34, 380 n. 6
Brown, G.   528 n. 12
Brown, R. E   269 n. 1
Brownlee, W. H.   347 n. 1, 466 n. 2, 474 n. 28
Brox, N.   305 n. 3
Buchanan, G. W.   421 n. 33, 795 n. 4
Buck, C. D.   524
Budde, K.   373 n. 30, 764 n. 11, 789 n. 62
Burney, C. F.   764 n. 11
Burrows, M.   323 n. 2
Burton, A.   828 n. 5

Cadell, H.   516 n. 10
Callaway, Ph.   117 n. 11
Cancik, H.   485 n. 7
Caquot, A.   220 n. 32
Carmignac, J.   3 n. 3, 795 nn. 3–4
Carnoy, A.   531 n. 23

Carr, D. 407 n. 29, 411 n. 41
Carrez, M. 243 n. 8
Carroll, R. P. 702 n. 6
Carson, D. A. 354 n. 24
Castro, F. P. 575 n. 11
Chaine, J. 258 n. 3
Charles, R. H. 261 n. 9, 782 n. 45
Charlesworth, J. H. 5 n. 9, 43 n. 3, 71 n. 3, 77 n. 16, 97 n. 1, 267 n. 25, 311 n. 18, 323 n. 3, 324 nn. 5, 7, 325 n. 8, 328 n. 18, 336 n. 1, 424 n. 43, 425 n. 45, 440 n. 11, 662 n. 2
Chavel, C. B. 258 n. 4
Chazon, E. G. 85 nn. 2, 5, 89 n. 11, 94 nn. 26–27, 121 n. 26, 180 n. 4, 207 n. 7, 317 n. 36
Chester, A. 151 n. 2
Childs, B. S. 64 n. 14
Chilton, B. 110 n. 51
Chyutin, M. 381 n. 7
Clarke, E. G. 263 n. 14
Cleaver-Bartholomew, D. 252 n. 43
Clements, R. 85 n. 5
Clifford, R. J. 844 n. 39
Clines, D. J. A. 720 n. 50
Cogan, M. 760 n. 3
Coggins, R. J. 308 n. 11
Cohen, M. 219 n. 28, 227 n. 68, 715 n. 36, 760 n. 4, 780 nn. 41, 43
Colera, P. B. 598 n. 19
Collins, A. Y. 129 n. 10
Collins, J. J. 91 n. 17, 150 n. 82, 151 n. 2, 206 n. 5, 308 n. 10, 324 n. 6, 331 n. 24, 424 n. 41, 425 n. 44, 431 n. 5, 479 n. 1, 796 n. 10, 797 n. 11
Collins, R. F. 269 n. 1
Colson, F. H. 283 n. 28, 821 n. 34

Cook E. C. 3 n. 5, 273 n. 16, 336 n. 1
Cook, E. M. 151 n. 2
Cook, J. 505 n. 23, 606 nn. 3, 5–9, 608 n. 14, 611 n. 21
Coppens, J. 619 n. 1
Cordoba 686 n. 4
Cortese, E. 736 n. 18
Cothenet, É. 3 n. 3
Cotton, H. M. 116 n. 8, 117 n. 11, 118 n. 14, 120 n. 24, 122 n. 30
Coulthard, M. 526 n. 6
Coupland, N. 526 n. 4
Cowley, A. E. 79 n. 21, 160 n. 8, 257 n. 1, 733 n. 7, 798 n. 17
Cox, C. E. 507 n. 27, 592 n. 5, 599 n. 20, 620 n. 4, 647
Craigie, P. C. 647
Crawford, T. G. 575 n. 10
Cross, F. M. 143 n. 58, 149 n. 80, 152 nn. 2–3, 153 n. 4, 182 n. 13, 216 n. 10, 219 n. 24, 220 n. 34, 221 n. 38, 224 n. 53, 228 n. 74, 372 n. 24, 375 n. 36, 404 n. 19, 416 n. 13, 439 n. 5, 440 n. 11, 446 n. 36, 468 n. 8, 677 n. 11, 735 n. 13, 767 n. 15
Crown, A. D. 160 n. 8, 215 nn. 5–6, 220 n. 31, 222 n. 44

Dahood, M. 647, 840 n. 21
Dalman, G. 371 n. 20
Danker F. W. 647
Daube, D. 230 n. 82
Davies, P. R. 106 n. 36, 425 n. 44
Davila, J. 137 n. 33
Dawson, D. A. 526 n. 4
Debrunner 261 n. 7
Deissmann, A. 560 n. 4
Delcor, M. 441 n. 17
Delisle, J. 643 n. 15

Delitzsch, F. 369 n. 10, 647
Denniston, J. D. 529 n. 15
Dévényi, K. 59 n. 8
Dietrich, M. 682 n. 25
Díez Macho, A. 264 n. 16
Di Lella, A. A. 279 n. 22, 308
   n. 11, 634 n. 2, 796 n. 6
Dillmann, A. 792 n. 66
Dillon, J. 100 n. 15
Dimant, D. 85 n. 4, 90 n. 13,
   121 n. 26, 316 n. 34, 380 n. 6,
   413 n. 1
Dorival, G. 524
Drijvers, H. J. W. 578 n. 19
Driver, G. R. 836 n. 9, 844 n. 34
Driver, S. R. 369 n. 10, 599
   n. 1, 756 n. 16, 805 n. 33
Duhaime, J. 28 n. 9
Dunand, F. 261 n. 6
Duncan, J. A. 228 n. 74, 449
   n. 45
Dupont-Sommer, A. 147 n. 72

Easton, R. L. 71 n. 3
Edgar, C. C. 537 n. 39
Eerdmans, B. D. 795 n. 4
Ehrlich, A. B. 789 n. 63, 834
   n. 2
Ehrman 686 n. 4
Eichler, B. L. 811 n. 1
Eisser, G. 831 n. 20
Elbogen, J. 833 n. 1
Eleazar L. 127 n. 1
Elliger, K. 347 n. 1, 745 n. 10
Ellington, J. 373 n. 29
Ellingworth, P. 368 n. 6
Elliott, J. K. 686 n. 4
Elman, Y. 55 n. 34
Elwolde, J. F. 138 n. 35
Emerton, J. A. 258 n. 4, 380
   n. 6, 737 n. 19
Engnell, I. 725 n. 5
Epstein, I. 766 n. 13, 780 n. 41
Epstein, J. N. 818 n. 26
Erbes, J. E. 578 n. 19

Eshel, E. 86 n. 7, 218 n. 20
Eshel, H. 118 n. 14, 129 n. 7,
   182 n. 13, 239 nn. 98, 100, 781
   n. 44
Eshkoli, A. Z. 826 n. 49
Eskhult, M. 527 n. 9
Etheridge, J. W. 818 n. 26
Evans, C. A. 265 n. 22, 328
   n. 18, 407 n. 29, 611 n. 21,
   760 n. 3
Eynikel, E. 524
Eyre, G. E. 822 n. 40
Fabry, H.-J. 180 n. 4, 242 n. 4,
   246 n. 22, 250 n. 39, 252 n. 49,
   313 n. 26, 317 n. 37

Fallon, F. 309 n. 15
Feldman, L. 470 n. 13, 661 n. 1
Field, F. 215 n. 2
Fields, K. E. 679 n. 18
Fields, W. 410 n. 37
Finegan, J. 161 n. 13
Finkelstein, J. J. 812 n. 6
Firmage, E. B. 831 n. 24
Fischer, B. 264 n. 17
Fishbane, M. 85 n. 4, 270 n. 7,
   298 n. 58, 354 n. 25, 364
   n. 55, 410 n. 37, 475 n. 33,
   755 n. 4
Fishwick, D. 726 n. 13
Fitzmyer, J. A. 43 n. 3, 151 n. 2,
   261 n. 6, 324 n. 5, 347 n. 2
Flashar M. 647
Fleischer, E. 722 n. 57
Fleming, D. E. 827 n. 2
Flint, P. W. 85 n. 2, 91 n. 15,
   98 n. 7, 128 n. 5, 138 n. 6,
   141 n. 47, 252 n. 45, 265 n. 20,
   270 n. 8, 277 n. 19, 297 n. 57,
   299 n. 61, 380 n. 5, 410 n. 39,
   448 n. 44, 592 n. 4, 647
Flower, B. 761 n. 6
Flusser, D. 151 n. 2
Folker, S. 284 n. 29
Forbes, A. D. 700 n. 3

Fox, M. V. 354 n. 26, 736 n. 15, 835 n. 4
Fraade, S. D. 54 n. 33
Fränkel, H. 761 n. 6
Frankel, Z. 216 n. 8
Frankfort, H. 726 n. 8
Frazer, J. G. 817 n. 19
Frazer, P. M. 828 n. 4
Freedman, D. N. 120 n. 25, 131 n. 13, 416 n. 13, 479 n. 1, 687 nn. 6, 8
Freudenthal, G. 718 n. 42
Frey, J. 313 n. 23, 380 n. 5
Fries, P. H. 529 n. 16
Fritz, V. 737 n. 18
Fröhlich, I. 59 n. 8
Fuller, R. E. 245 n. 17, 246 n. 21
Funk 261 n. 7

Gafni, I. 53 n. 30
Gall, A. von 779 n. 39
García Martínez, F. 10 n. 14, 52 n. 26, 76 n. 12, 81, 105 n. 33, 119 n. 20, 149 n. 81, 151-152 n. 2, 252 n. 44, 292 n. 47, 331 n. 24, 332 n. 27, 336 n. 1, 379 n. 1, 380 n. 5, 391 n. 26, 424 n. 41, 796 n. 8, 822 n. 37
Gardiner, A. H. 726 n. 10
Garfinkel, S. P. 624 n. 20
Garsiel, M. 768 n. 16
Gaster, M. 159 n. 3
Gaston, L. 258 n. 4
Geiger, A. 373 n. 28, 759 n. 3
Geiger, J. 122 n. 30
Geller, S. A. 675 n. 1
Gemser, B. 834 n. 2
Gentry, P. J. 507 n. 27
Gese, H. 745 n. 10
Gesenius, W. 79 n. 21, 216 n. 7, 257 n. 1
Gevirtz, M. L. 804 n. 31
Gichon, M. 223 n. 48
Giglioli, P. P. 642 n. 13

Gingrich, F. W. 647
Ginsberg, H. L. 785 n. 53
Ginsburg, C. D. 367 n. 1
Ginzberg, L. 467 n. 5
Gitin, S. 205 n. 4, 368 n. 4, 421 n. 32
Glazier, M. 468 n. 7
Gmirkin, R. 29 n. 10
Goitein, S. D. 787 n. 60
Golb, N. 56 n. 38, 206 n. 5
Goldin, J. 814 n. 11
Goldstein, J. A. 281 n. 26, 820 n. 30
Good, E. M. 244 n. 14
Gooding, D. W. 626 n. 33
Goodman, M. 97 n. 4, 100 n. 14, 145 n. 67, 309 n. 14, 479 n. 1
Gordis, R. 778 n. 37
Goshen-Gottstein, M. H. 451 n. 49
Gray, G. B. 676 n. 5, 756 n. 16
Green, D. 224 n. 58
Green, W. S. 350 n. 12
Greenberg, M. 621 n. 7, 711 n. 23, 748 n. 34
Greenblatt, C. 72 n. 7
Greenfell, B. P. 551 n. 1
Greenfield, J. C. 312 n. 21, 416 n. 13, 429 n. 1, 431 nn. 4-5
Greenspoon, L. 599 n. 21, 620 n. 4
Grillet, B. 625 n. 27
Grimes, J. E. 526 n. 4
Grintz, Y. M. 225 n. 63, 760 n. 5
Grossman, A. 714 n. 34
Gunkel, H. 258 n. 3, 725 n. 2
Gunn, D. 687 n. 6
Gurock, J. 55 n. 34
Güterbock, H. G. 734 n. 9
Gütersloh 620 n. 4

Haak, R. D. 244 n. 15
Habermann, A. M. 341 n. 15

Hachlili, R.   223 n. 47
Haelst, J. van   570 n. 8
Hahn, D.   143 n. 55
Hahn, F.   263 n. 11
Hall, J. R. C.   822 n. 40
Halliday, M. A. K.   529 n. 16
Hallo, W. W.   755 n. 4
Halperin, D.   93 n. 24
Halpern, B.   120 n. 25, 131 n. 13
Hammershaimb, E.   802 n. 26
Hänel, J.   769 n. 17
Hanhart, R.   506 n. 25
Hanson, J.   307 n. 8
Hanson, R. S.   224 n. 57
Haran, M.   238 n. 93, 785 n. 54
Harl, M.   524, 525 n. 2, 530
    n. 20, 620 n. 4
Harrington, D.   207 n. 7, 578
    n. 21, 662 n. 2
Harrington, H. K.   131 n. 14
Harris, R.   811 n. 4
Harrison, C. R.   243 n. 11
Hartman, L. E.   796 n. 6
Hata, G.   470 n. 13
Hatch, E.   594 n. 12
Hauret, Ch.   774 n. 30
Hauspie, K.   524
Hayman, A. P.   578 n. 19
Heckel, U.   151 n. 2
Heerma van Voss, M. S. H. G.
    436 n. 15
Heinemann, J.   91 n. 18
Held, M.   734 n. 9
Helfmeyer, F. J.   796 n. 10
Hellholm, D.   325 n. 10, 425
    n. 44
Hempel, C.   98 n. 8, 99 n. 13,
    107 n. 37, 130 n. 12, 131
    n. 13, 132 n. 15, 149 n. 81,
    206 n. 6, 321 n. 42
Hendel, R. S.   462 n. 18, 730
    n. 2, 790 n. 65
Hengel, M.   151 n. 2, 325 nn.
    10–11, 333 n. 29, 620 n. 5
Henshke, D.   54 n. 31

Herschbell, J.   100 n. 15
Hertzberg, H. W.   369 n. 10
Heschel, A. J.   819 n. 26
Hiebert, R, J, V.   507 n. 27
Hirschberg, H. Z.   796 n. 10
Hirschfeld, H.   816 n. 18
Hoffer, V.   735 n. 15
Hoffner, H. A.   829 n. 8
Hoftijzer, J.   797 n. 13
Holladay, C. R.   307 n. 9
Holladay, W. L.   702 n. 5
Hollander, H. W.   429 n. 1
Holmes   686 n. 4
Holzinger, H.   792 n. 67
Horgan, M. P.   347 n. 1, 466
    n. 4
Horovitz, H. S.   814 n. 11
Horst, F.   802 n. 26
Hospers, J. H.   578 n. 19
Houwink ten Cate, Ph. H. J.   436
    n. 15
Howard, G.   508 n. 29
Hübsch, A.   717 n. 40
Humbert, J.   529 n. 15
Hunt, A. S.   537 n. 39, 551 n. 1
Hurowitz, V.   138 n. 35
Hurtado, L. W.   58 n. 6

Ibn Ganah   757 n. 18
Ilan, T.   132 n. 18, 142 n. 49,
    225 n. 63
Isaksson, A.   133 n. 20
Isenberg, H.   526 n. 6
Iványi, T.   59 n. 8
Iwry, S.   806 n. 35

Jack, A.   58 n. 6
Jacobsen, E.   643 n. 15
Jacobson, H.   309 n. 14, 662 n. 3
James, M. R.   661 n. 1
Janzen, J. G.   702 n. 5
Japhet, S.   710 n. 18, 719 n. 45,
    720 n. 49, 722 n. 55, 757 n. 20,
    797 n. 14
Jastram, N.   227 n. 71

Jastrow, M. 800 n. 21
Jaworski, A. 526 n. 4
Jay, N. 679, 677 n. 14
Jean, C. F. 797 n. 13
Jellicoe, S. 497 n. 2
Jellinek, A. 431 n. 6, 719 n. 46
Jenni, E. 795 n. 2
Jeremias, G. 421 n. 33, 468 n. 7
Jobes, K. H. 524, 620 n. 4
Joeshen, T. 734 n. 9
Johnston, R. H. 71 n. 3
Jones, B. A. 243 n. 10
Jones, H. S. 639 n. 11, 647
Jonge, M. de 429 n. 1, 435 n. 15
Joüon, P. 79 n. 21, 257 n. 1,
    341 n. 16, 734 n. 8

Kahila, G. 72 n. 7
Kahle, P. 114 n. 4, 216 n. 9
Kaiser, C. 620 n. 4
Kaiser, O. 308 n. 11
Kalimi, I. 770 n. 21
Kallai, Z. 783 n. 49
Kallmeyer, W. 526 n. 6
Kamin, S. 711 n. 22, 713 n. 30
Kampen, J. I. 66 n. 17, 119
    n. 20, 149 n. 81, 299 n. 61
Kapera, Z. J. 323 n. 3
Kasher, M. M. 818 n. 26
Kataja, L. 830 n. 11
Kaufmann, Y. 725 n. 6
Kautzsch, E. 79 n. 21, 647, 257
    n. 1
Kedar-Kopfstein, B. 593 n. 7
Keil, C. F. 369 n. 10, 647
Kellermann, D. 721 n. 51
Kelley, P. H. 575 n. 10
Kelly, L. 640 n. 12
Kelner, M. 718 n. 42
Kenyon, F. 700 n. 3
Kimchi, R. D. 757 n. 19
Kister, M. 147 n. 72
Kittel, B. 85 n. 4
Klauck, H. J. 100 n. 15
Klein, R. W. 462 n. 18

Klijn, A. F. J. 667 n. 6
Klinghardt, M. 98 n. 10
Kloppenborg, J. S. 100 n. 14
Knibb, M. A. 55 n. 35, 252
    n. 47
Knight, K. 817 n. 22
Knohl, I. 743 n. 4
Knox, K. T. 71 n. 3
Koehler 79 n. 22
Kohn, S. 216 n. 8
Kollmann, B. 53 n. 27, 468
    n. 10
Komlosh, Y. 708 n. 8
König, E. 258 n. 3
Kooij, A. van der 731 n. 3, 737
    n. 19, 738 n. 21
Koole, J. L. 734 n. 10
Kosmala, H. 795 n. 4
Kosmala, L. 423 n. 36
Krasovac, J. 159 n. 2, 620 n. 4
Kraeling, E. G. 798 n. 17
Kratz, R. G. 778 n. 37
Kraus, H.-J. 647
Kress, G. 529 n. 16
Kroeken, M. 528 n. 12
Kuenen, W. 747 n. 26, 792
    n. 66
Kugel, J. 85 n. 5, 409 n. 36,
    429 n. 3
Kugler, R. A. 150 n. 82, 212
    n. 16
Kuhl C. 808 n. 40
Kuhn, K. G. 57 n. 4, 327 n. 16,
    424 n. 43
Kutscher, E. Y. 313 n. 25, 381
    n. 8, 445 n. 30, 787 n. 60
Kvalbein, H. 331 n. 24

Labov, W. 527 n. 8
Lagrange, M.-J. 786 n. 58
Lambert, W. G. 682 n. 24
Landmesser, C. 321 n. 42
Lane, D. J. 578 n. 19
Langdon, S. H. 756 n. 12
Lange, A. 180 n. 4, 206 n. 6,

252 n. 46, 306 n. 6, 313 nn. 23, 26, 317 n. 37
Lange, N. de   712 n. 23
Lapp, N. L.   224 n. 53
Lapp, P. W.   224 n. 53
Larson, E. W.   102 n. 20, 115 n. 7, 124 n. 36, 317 n. 39
LaSor, W. S.   424 n. 43
Laurin, R. B.   424 n. 43
Lauterbach, J. Z.   710 n. 18, 814 n. 11
Le Boulluec, A.   517 n. 12, 524, 530 n. 20
Leaney, A. R. C.   336 n. 1
Lebrecht, F.   757 n. 19
LeDéaut, R.   409 n. 35, 818 n. 26
Lee, J. A. L.   524
Leeuwen, R. C. van   846 n. 44
Lefevere, A.   635 n. 3
Leiman, S. Z.   271 n. 8, 368 n. 2
Léon, D. M.   379 n. 1
Lestienne, M.   625 n. 27
Levey, S. H.   623 n. 17
Levine, B. A.   414 n. 3, 676 n. 5, 824 n. 48
Levine, L. I.   58 n. 7, 223 n. 49
Lewy, J.   374 n. 30, 404 n. 17, 831 n. 20
Licht, J.   4 n. 7, 336 n. 4, 382 n. 11, 822 n. 37
Lichtenberger, H.   180 n. 4, 206 n. 6, 252 n. 46, 313 n. 26, 317 n. 37, 323 n. 3, 324 nn. 5, 7, 328 n. 18, 485 n. 7
Lichtheim, M.   823 n. 42
Liddell, H. G.   639 n. 11, 647
Lieberman, S.   102 n. 21, 225 n. 62, 367 n. 2, 418 n. 21, 817 n. 19
Lightstone, J. N.   275 n. 17
Lignée, H.   3 n. 3
Lim, T. H.   58 n. 6, 71 n. 2, 182 n. 13, 460 n. 16
Littmann, E.   782 n. 45

Liver, J.   48 n. 17, 417 n. 17, 424 n. 43
Liwak, R.   783 n. 49
Lloyd-Jones, H.   659
Lockshin, M. L.   722 n. 58
Loewe, R. J.   709 n. 15
Loewenstamm, S. E.   746 n. 15, 765 n. 12, 807 n. 38
Lohfink, N. F.   745 n. 10
Lohse, E.   336 n. 1
Longacre, R. E.   527 nn. 7–8, 528 n. 11
Louw, J. P.   524
Lowery, K. E.   526 n. 4
Lown, Philip L.   52 n. 26
Lundberg, M. J.   439 n. 7
Lundbom, J.   687 n. 8
Lust, J.   524, 619 n. 1
Luzzatto, S. D.   825
Lyall, F.   815 n. 13

Maarsingh, B.   621 n. 7, 622 n. 13
Macdonald, J.   215 n. 4
Macholz, Chr.   804 n. 30
Macintosh, A. A.   784 n. 51
Magen, Y.   222 n. 42, 314 n. 30, 779 n. 40
Magness, J. L.   97 n. 1, 98 n. 7, 140 n. 43, 141 n. 47, 142 n. 50, 148 n. 78, 421 n. 32
Maharzu   820 n. 33
Maher, M.   263 n. 15, 819 n. 26
Maier, J.   82 n. 35, 248 n. 32, 380 n. 6, 382 n. 12
Manns, F.   314 n. 30
Marcos, N. F.   591 n. 2, 594 n. 11, 597 n. 17, 603 n. 24
Marcus, R.   422 n. 35, 469 n. 11
Margulies, M   35 n. 3, 818 n. 26
Marquis, G.   212 n. 17
Martin, J.   369 n. 10
Martin, M.   440 n. 14
Mason, S.   286 n. 34, 470 n. 13
Mass, P.   761 n. 6

Mateos 686 n. 4
Mathews, H. J. 723 n. 59
Mattila, S. L. 151 n. 2
Mayer, G. 246 n. 22
Mazar, B. 226 n. 65, 746 n. 15
Mazor, L. 588 n. 29, 772 n. 25
McCarter, P. K. 370 nn. 13–14
McCarthy, D. J. 676 n. 4
McDonald, L. M. 275 n. 17, 408 n. 34
McKane, W. 367 n. 2, 610 n. 20, 701 n. 4, 836 n. 9
McLean, M. D. 224 n. 59
McLean, N. 372 n. 25, 563 n. 5, 571 n. 2
McNally 97 n. 1, 148 n. 78
McNamara, M. 819 n. 26
McNutt, P. 687 n. 6
Medico, H. del 123 n. 32
Meer, M. N. van der 584 n. 24
Meeteren, N. van 242 n. 2
Meier, J. 469 n. 10
Melamed, E. Z. 367 n. 1, 709 n. 15, 818 n. 26, 835 n. 4
Merdler, R. 722 n. 56
Metso, S. 108 n. 43, 149 n. 79, 452 n. 52
Metzger, B. M. 815 n. 14
Meyer, R. 575 n. 8
Milgrom, J. 79 n. 24, 358 nn. 36–37, 361 n. 47, 743 n. 3, 744 n. 6, 746 n. 16, 748 n. 34, 749 n. 1, 823 n. 44, 824 n. 48
Milik, J. T. 3 n. 2, 20 n. 3, 29 n. 12, 57 n. 4, 116 n. 9, 138 n. 36, 144 n. 62, 151 nn. 1–2, 153 n. 4, 180 n. 6, 182 n. 13, 224 n. 56, 228 n. 76, 247 n. 31, 294 n. 51, 297 n. 55, 309 n. 16, 379 n. 1, 382 n. 11, 429 n. 1, 432 n. 8, 439 n. 2, 466 n. 4
Millar, F. 309 n. 14, 479 n. 1
Miller, L. 766 n. 13

Milligan, G. 647
Mirkin, M. 821 n. 33
Mittmann-Richert, U. 306 n. 6
Moberly, R. W. L. 258 n. 4
Mojola, A. 368 n. 6
Mölle, H. 258 n. 4
Montaner, L. V. 97 n. 3, 128 n. 5, 129 n. 8, 295 n. 54, 299 n. 61, 347 n. 4, 351 n. 13, 457 n. 9
Montevecchi, O. 647
Montgomery, J. A. 222 n. 43
Moore, C. A. 308 n. 12
Moran, W. L. 830 n. 15
Morgenstern, M. 312 n. 21
Moshqovitz, Y. Ts. 744 n. 6
Mosis, R. 258 n. 4, 261 n. 8
Motzkin, G. 53 n. 30
Moulton, J. H. 647
Mowinckel, S. 725 n. 3, 752 n. 43
Moxnes, H. 262 n. 10
Mozley, F. W. 647
Mulder, M. J. 85 n. 4, 298 n. 58, 354 n. 27, 369 n. 9, 497 n. 3
Müller, W. W. 721 n. 53
Munnich, O. 524, 599 n. 21, 620 n. 4
Muraoka, T. 79 n. 21, 138 n. 35, 243 n. 9, 312 n. 21, 336 n. 3, 338 n. 7, 341 n. 16, 342 n. 20, 524, 647, 734 n. 8
Murphy, C. M. 98 n. 9, 378 n. 46, 595 n. 12
Murphy, F. J. 662 n. 3, 667 n. 6
Murphy, R. E. 815 n. 14
Murphy-O'Connor, J. 106 nn. 35–36, 739 n. 23
Mynatt, D. S. 575 n. 10

Na'aman, N. 783 n. 49
Naeh, S. 827 n. 2
Nautin, P. 113 n. 1

Naveh, J.   222 n. 42, 223 n. 47, 225 n. 63, 226 n. 65, 840 n. 20
Nebe, H. W.   247 n. 26
Neeman, Y.   226 n. 65
Negev, A.   381 n. 7
Netzer, E.   317 n. 38
Neusner, J.   110 n. 51, 470 n. 13
Newman, C.   120 n. 23
Newman, J. H.   85 n. 4
Newsom, C. A.   94 n. 29, 120 n. 25, 179, 312 n. 19, 317 n. 37, 349 nn. 8–9, 425 n. 44
Niccacci, A.   527 n. 7, 532 n. 25
Nida, E. A.   524
Nitzan, B.   91 n. 17, 347 n. 1, 352 n. 19, 465 n. 1, 473 n. 23
Nixon, P.   812 n. 7
Noort, E.   391 n. 26
Nougayrol, J.   813 n. 9

O'Callaghan, M. J.   129 n. 9
O'Connor, M.   79 n. 21, 80 n. 26, 257 n. 1
Oegema, G. S.   323 n. 3, 324 n. 5, 324 n. 7, 328 n. 18
Oehming, M.   258 n. 4
Oesch, J. M.   160 n. 4
Offerhaus, U.   242 n. 4
Olyan, S.   440 n. 10
Opelt, I.   368 n. 5
Ophuizen, J. M. van   528 n. 10
Oppenheim, A. L.   681 n. 23
Oppenheimer, A.   102 n. 21
Overton, S. D.   687 n. 6

Pardee, D. G.   206 n. 5
Parpola, S.   831 n. 17
Parry, D. W.   15 n. 26, 36 n. 5, 72 n. 7, 108 n. 43, 119 n. 20, 152 n. 2, 332 n. 24, 372 n. 24, 442 nn. 20, 23
Pasquali, G.   759 n. 1
Paul, A.   114 n. 4, 368 n. 4, 373 n. 29
Paul, S. M.   367 n. 1, 757 n. 20, 801 n. 23, 831 n. 24

Paulsen, H.   333 n. 29
Pelletier, A.   524
Perrin, B.   813 n. 9
Perrot, C.   354 n. 27
Person, R. F.   735 n. 13
Pettinato, G.   682 n. 25
Pfann, S. J.   107 n. 39, 119 n. 18
Philonenko, M.   220 n. 32
Pietersma, A.   508 n. 28, 599 n. 20, 629 n. 41, 637 n. 8, 647
Pinnick, A.   85 n. 5
Pintaudi, R.   571 n. 1
Pisano, S.   592 n. 6
Pliny   97 n. 5
Ploeg, van der J.   28 n. 8
Polak, F.   535 n. 35
Pope, M. H.   377 n. 42, 756 n. 15
Porath, Y.   226 n. 65
Porter, S. E.   12 n. 20
Poznanski, S.   714 n. 34
Price, J. J.   120 n. 24
Priest, J.   422 n. 35
Pritchard, J. B.   844 n. 35
Propp, W. H.   120 n. 25, 131 n. 13
Puech, É.   179, 180 n. 5, 213 n. 20, 250 n. 38, 311 n. 18, 316 n. 33, 331 n. 24, 332 n. 25, 380 n. 6, 392 n. 29, 441 n. 17, 475 n. 34, 769 n. 18
Pummer, R.   222 n. 44
Purvis, J. D.   221 n. 39

Qimron, E.   47 n. 14, 54 n. 31, 74, 128 n. 5, 179 n. 3, 312 n. 21, 344 n. 22, 350 n. 11, 361 n. 44, 416 n. 9, 444 n. 28, 769 n. 18
Quentin, H.   264 n. 18

Raamattu, P.   508 n. 30
Rabin, C.   261 n. 9, 418 n. 21
Rabin, I. A.   814 n. 11
Rabinowitz, I. L.   347 n. 1, 367 n. 1

Rad, G. von 257 n. 2, 258 n. 3
Rahlfs, A. 545 n. 4, 553 n. 2, 560 n. 4, 563 n. 5, 577 n. 16, 591 n. 1
Ramp, J. 143 n. 56
Rappaport, U. 121 n. 26
Ratner, R. J. 804 n. 31
Ratzahbi, J. 802 n. 24
Redpath, H. A. 594 n. 12
Reed, S. A. 439 n. 7
Reeves, J. C. 66 n. 17, 311 n. 18
Regt, L. J. de. 531 n. 22
Reinbold, W. 468 n. 10
Reisner, G. A. 374 n. 32
Reventlow, H. G. 620 n. 4
Richards, K. H. 267 n. 25
Richland, N. 311 n. 18
Ricks, S. D. 72 n. 7, 152 n. 2, 442 n. 20
Rietzschel, C. 702 n. 6
Rijksbaron, A. 529 nn. 13, 15
Ringgren, H. 725 n. 4
Robert, U. 578 n. 18
Roberts, C. H. 121 n. 27
Roberts, J. J. M. 726 n. 11
Robertson, A. T. 647
Robertson, R. G. 309 n. 14
Robinson, D. 635 n. 3
Robinson, Th. R. 802 n. 26
Rofé, A. 63 n. 13, 354 n. 26, 737 n. 20, 759 n. 3, 762 n. 7, 764 n. 11, 770 n. 20, 778 n. 37, 789 n. 64, 792 n. 69
Röhrer-Ertl, O. 143 n. 55
Rohrhirsch, F. 143 n. 55
Roifer, A. 778 n. 37
Roo, J. C. R. de 12 n. 20
Rösel, M. 790 n. 65
Rosenbloom, N. H. 826 n. 49
Rosenthal, E. S. 225 n. 63
Rosenzweig, A. 833 n. 1
Rosin, D. 719 n. 45
Roth, M. E. 831 nn. 21–22
Rothstein, J. W. 769 n. 17
Rottzoll, D. U. 258 n. 4
Rowley, H. H. 114 n. 4

Royce, J. R. 686 n. 4
Rudolph, W. 702 n. 6
Rüger, H. P. 745 n. 10
Russo, C. F. 761 n. 6
Rynell, A. 526 n. 5

Sabatier, P. 578 n. 17
Sabin, P. 29 n. 10
Sacks, R. D. 258 n. 3
Saebo, M. 284 n. 29
Sáenz-Badillos A. 603 n. 24
Safrai, Z. 223 n. 47
Saiz, J. R. B. 591 n. 2, 594 n. 11, 599 n. 21
Saldarini, A. J. 578 n. 21
Salters, R. B. 719 n. 45
Saltman, A. 710 n. 18
Sanders, E. 470 n. 13
Sanders, J. A. 90 n. 14, 91 n. 15, 275 n. 17, 295 n. 53, 398 n. 7, 405 nn. 23–24, 406 n. 25, 408 nn. 33–34, 410 n. 37
Sanderson, J. E. 165 n. 22, 180 n. 7, 219 n. 23
Sandevoir, P. 517 n. 12, 524, 530 n. 20
Sarason, R. S. 91 n. 18
Sarna, N. M. 258 n. 3
Sasson, V. 727 n. 14
Satlow, M. L. 137 n. 33
Sawyer J. F. A. 640 n. 12
Schäfer, P. 485 n. 7
Schaper, J. 620 n. 5
Schiffman, L. H. 4 n. 9, 43 n. 3, 55 n. 35, 58 n. 7, 64 n. 15, 90 n. 13, 94 n. 27, 97 n. 3, 101 n. 18, 110 n. 50, 114 n. 4, 119 n. 21, 127 n. 1, 128 nn. 5–6, 131 n. 14, 146 n. 70, 212 n. 17, 292 n. 49, 316 n. 34, 350 n. 12, 351 n. 14, 362 n. 49, 363 n. 51, 380 nn. 5–6, 398 n. 7, 413 n. 1, 414 nn. 2, 7, 416 n. 8, 417 n. 17, 419 n. 25, 421 n. 32, 424 nn. 42–43, 425 nn. 44–45,

426 n. 49, 441 n. 17, 447 n. 41,
    453 n. 2, 466 n. 1, 475 n. 33,
    479 n. 1, 739 n. 23
Schiffrin, D.   526 n. 4
Schmidt, C.   560 n. 4
Schmidt, J. H. H.   524
Schniedewind, W. M.   15 n. 26
Scholem, G.   432 n. 9
Schoors, A.   207 n. 7
Schorr, M.   811 n. 4
Schreiber, S.   323 n. 3
Schrenk, G.   271 n. 10
Schuller, E. M.   49 n. 19, 85
    n. 3, 86 n. 7, 89 n. 11, 91
    n. 17, 95 n. 32, 104 n. 28,
    128 n. 5, 138 n. 6, 207 n. 7
Schürer, E.   479 n. 1
Schwartz, B. J.   741 n. 2, 782
    n. 46, 830 n. 14
Schwartz, D. R.   53 n. 30, 325
    n. 10, 416 n. 12
Schwemer, A. M.   620 n. 5
Scorgie, G.   685 n. 3
Scott, J. M.   313 n. 23
Scott, R.   639 n. 11, 647
Seebass, H.   796 n. 10
Seeligmann, I. L.   759 n. 3, 818
    n. 23, 838 n. 13
Segal, M.   351 n. 14
Sereni, E.   763 n. 9
Seybold, K.   249 n. 36
Shehadeh, H.   160 n. 8
Shemesh, A.   356 n. 32
Sheridan, S.   143 n. 56
Shiro, M.   526 n. 6
Sicking, C. M. J.   528 n. 10
Siegel, J.   440 n. 15
Silberman, L.   424 n. 43
Silberman, N. A.   97 n. 3, 127
    n. 1
Silva M.   524, 620 n. 4
Simon, U.   760 n. 4
Sinclair, L. A.   247 n. 27
Sint, J. A.   305 n. 3

Sipilä, S.   505 n. 23, 606 nn. 7, 9
Sivan, D.   312 n. 21
Skehan, P. W.   94 n. 29, 165
    n. 22, 180 n. 7, 219 n. 23, 224
    n. 58, 279 n. 22, 308 n. 11,
    402, 441 n. 17, 634 n. 2
Slotki, I. W.   371 n. 19
Slotki, J. J.   371 n. 22
Smalley, W.   367 n. 2
Smend, R.   774 n. 31
Smith, M.   441 n. 18
Smith, P.   72 n. 7, 225 n. 63
Smith, W. R.   676, 677 n. 10
Smyth, H. W.   647
Sokoloff, M.   205 n. 4, 368 n. 4
Sollamo, R.   497 n. 1, 504 n. 20,
    505 n. 23, 506 n. 26, 606 n. 7
Söllner, P.   382 n. 12
Sommer, B. D.   95 n. 31
Somolinos, J. R.   598 n. 19
Southwood, C. H.   734 n. 12
Sparks, H. F. D.   708 n. 7
Spector, J.   162 n. 15
Sperber, A.   263 n. 12
Speyer, W.   305 n. 3
Spottiswoode, A.   822 n. 40
Spronk, K.   248 n. 34
Staerk, W.   795 n. 4
Starcky, J.   382 n. 14, 404 n. 20,
    425 n. 44
Steck, O. H.   245 n. 18, 305
    n. 4
Steckoll   143 n. 53
Stegemann, E.   804 n. 30
Stegemann, H.   4 n. 6, 97 n. 3,
    99 n. 12, 128 n. 5, 129 n. 8,
    253 n. 50, 380 n. 6, 392 n. 30,
    414 n. 3, 425 n. 44, 441 n. 17,
    470 n. 15
Steiner, R. C.   312 n. 22, 712
    n. 23
Stemberger, G.   468 n. 10
Steudel, A.   107 n. 40, 195 n. 34,
    251 n. 41, 316 n. 35, 332

n. 27, 468 n. 10, 472 n. 22,
796 n. 5
Stiehl, R.   313 n. 25
Stipp, H. J.   731 n. 3
Stone, M. E.   89 n. 11, 180 n. 4,
207 n. 7, 317 n. 36, 429 nn.
1–2, 431 nn. 4–5, 665 n. 5, 780
n. 42
Strauß, H.   246 n. 22
Streane, A. W.   702 n. 5
Streck, M.   756 n. 10
Strobel, A.   244 n. 16
Strugnell, J.   44 n. 3, 54 n. 31,
71 n. 2, 132 n. 17, 181 n. 10,
201 n. 40, 206 n. 6, 219 n. 27,
316 n. 35, 361 n. 44, 379 n. 1,
416 n. 9, 442 n. 22
Stuckenbruck, L. T.   5 n. 9, 311
n. 18, 323 n. 3
Sutcliffe, E. F.   99 n. 11
Svend Holm-Nielsen   85 n. 3
Szondy, P.   349 n. 10

Tadmor, H.   785 n. 54, 829 n. 7
Tailor, L. R.   726 n. 13
Tal, A.   164 n. 18, 217 n. 16
Talmage, F. E.   716 n. 39
Talmon, S.   52 n. 26, 124 n. 35,
180 n. 7, 220 n. 34, 265 n. 22,
404 n. 19, 407 n. 29, 417 nn.
14–15, 423 n. 41, 446 n. 36,
453 nn. 1–2, 591 n. 3, 611
n. 21, 645 n. 1, 735 n. 13, 760
n. 3, 767 n. 15, 778 n. 37, 795
n. 4, 804 nn. 30–31, 808 n. 40,
833 n. 1, 839 n. 15
Talshir, Z.   592 n. 5
Tantlevskij, I. R.   249 n. 37
Ta-Shma, Y. M.   712 n. 23, 722
n. 57, 809 n. 43
Taylor, B. A.   606 n. 6, 620 n. 4
Taylor, J.   142 n. 48
Thackeray, H. J.   372 n. 25, 647,
699 n. 1

Thenius, O.   373 n. 30, 591 n. 1
Thiede, C. P.   129 n. 9
Thompson, Y.   719 n. 46
Thomson, J. E. H.   217 n. 18
Thrall, M. E.   530 n. 21
Tigay, J. H.   702 n. 6, 737 n. 20,
813 n. 9
Tigchelaar, E. J. C.   76 n. 12, 81,
252 n. 44, 332 n. 27, 336 n. 1,
796 n. 8
Timpanaro, S.   759 n. 1
Tobin, T. H.   91 n. 17, 431 n. 5,
797 n. 11
Toeg, A.   231 n. 85
Torczyner, N. H.   833 n. 1
Tov, E.   57 nn. 2–3, 59 n. 10, 83
n. 38, 94 n. 27, 115 n. 6, 119
nn. 18, 21, 159 n. 2, 180 n. 4,
180 n. 6, 207 n. 7, 212 n. 17,
216 n. 13, 218 n. 20, 220 nn.
29–31, 238 n. 92, 242 n. 2, 243
n. 12, 256 n. 52, 270 n. 7, 293
n. 50, 313 n. 27, 316 n. 36, 347
n. 4, 351 n. 14, 369 n. 11, 380
n. 5, 384 n. 18, 410 n. 37, 439
n. 1, 441 n. 17, 442 nn. 20, 23,
454 n. 3, 462 n. 20, 497 n. 3,
507 n. 27, 509 n. 31, 511
n. 33, 586 n. 28, 597 n. 18,
599 n. 20, 605 n. 1, 606 n. 4,
608 n. 15, 645 n. 1, 685 n. 1,
702 n. 6, 729, 733 n. 6, 759
n. 3, 835 n. 3
Toy, C. H.   834 n. 2
Treat, J. C.   721 n. 52
Tromp, J.   731 n. 4
Troyer, K. de   571 n. 1
Tsevat, M.   374 n. 30, 760 n. 5
Tsifroni, A.   816 n. 18
Tucket, C. M.   620 n. 4
Turner, E. G.   121 n. 28, 515
n. 8, 563 n. 6
Tur-Sinai, N. H.   756 n. 16, 774
n. 32, 836 n. 8, 842 n. 28

Twersky, I.   817 n. 19
Tzaferis, V.   225 n. 61

Uchelen, N. A. van   436 n. 15
Uffenheimer, B.   765 n. 12
Ullinger, J.   143 n. 56
Ulrich, E. C.   15 n. 26, 36 n. 5,
    92 n. 19, 108 n. 43, 165 n. 22,
    180 n. 7, 219 nn. 23, 25, 227
    n. 71, 228 n. 74, 252 n. 45,
    265 n. 20, 270 n. 7, 292 n. 49,
    332 n. 24, 347 n. 4, 351 n. 13,
    372 n. 24, 373 n. 28, 414
    n. 2, 441 n. 16, 442 n. 23,
    460 n. 16, 498 n. 5, 592 n. 4,
    735 n. 13, 772 n. 26
Urbach, E. E.   719 n. 47
Utzschneider, H.   242 nn. 3–4

VanderKam, J. C.   52 nn. 26–27,
    55 n. 35, 85 n. 2, 94 n. 27, 97
    nn. 2–3, 98 n. 7, 114 n. 4, 117
    n. 12, 119 n. 21, 127 n. 1, 128
    nn. 5–6, 131 n. 14, 138 n. 6,
    141 n. 47, 144 n. 64, 212 n. 17,
    220 n. 29, 265 n. 22, 267 n. 25,
    279 n. 23, 292 n. 49, 294
    n. 51, 295 n. 54, 297 n. 57,
    347 n. 4, 351 n. 14, 362 nn.
    49–50, 380 n. 5, 398 n. 7, 414
    n. 2, 441 n. 17, 448 n. 44, 453
    n. 2, 457 n. 9, 466 n. 1, 479
    n. 1, 498 n. 5, 739 n. 23
Vaux, R. de   98 n. 6, 114 n. 3,
    116 n. 9, 118 n. 17, 127 n. 3,
    180 n. 6, 228 n. 76, 417 n. 16
Vermes, G.   3 n. 4, 23 n. 5, 25
    n. 7, 82 n. 34, 97 n. 4, 101
    n. 17, 108 n. 43, 128 n. 4, 133
    n. 19, 145 n. 67, 149 n. 81,
    292 n. 48, 306 n. 5, 309 n. 14,
    328 n. 17, 336 n. 1, 347 n. 2,
    443 n. 27, 466 n. 3, 479 n. 1,
    480 n. 2, 707 n. 6, 708 n. 7
Vincent, L. H.   223 n. 48

Vliet, W. M. van   578 n. 19
Volz, P.   479 n. 1
Vriezen, Th. C.   805 n. 33

Waard, J. de   368 n. 6
Wacholder, B. Z.   208 n. 10, 266
    n. 23, 379 n. 2, 476 n. 36
Wagner, S.   783 n. 49
Walfisch. B. D.   719 n. 46
Walker-Ramisch, S.   102 n. 20
Walters, P.   626 n. 33
Waltke, B. K.   79 n. 21, 80 n. 26,
    257 n. 1
Walton, B.   578 n. 21
Wassen, C.   128 n. 5
Watanabe, K.   831 n. 17
Watson, W. G. E.   822 n. 37
Weber, R.   578 n. 20
Weil, G. E.   575 n. 10
Weinberg, J. J.   231 n. 86
Weinert, F. D.   43 n. 3
Weinfeld, M.   90 n. 13, 98 n. 9,
    414 n. 7, 713 n. 30, 813 n. 9,
    827 n. 1, 830 n. 13, 831 n. 18,
    842 n. 27
Weingreen, J.   836 n. 7
Weiser, A.   647
Weiss, M.   782 n. 47, 801 n. 23
Weiss, R.   216 n. 12, 219 n. 27,
    407 n. 29, 759 n. 2, 780 n. 42
Wellhausen, J.   375 n. 34, 762
    n. 8, 792 n. 66
Westbrook, R.   811 n. 1
Westermann, C.   258 n. 3
Wevers, J. W.   260 n. 5, 509
    n. 32, 524, 525 n. 2, 530 n. 18,
    541 nn. 1–2
Whitaker, G. H.   821 n. 34
White, R. T.   82 n. 35
White, S. C.   76 n. 12, 124 n. 36,
    135 n. 28, 219 n. 25, 220 nn.
    29–30, 347 n. 4, 351 n. 13, 379
    n. 1, 384 n. 18
Whiting, R.   830 n. 11
Whybray, R. N.   840 n. 23

Wicksteed, P. H.   747 n. 26
Wieder, N.   55 n. 35
Wiener, H. M.   808 n. 40
Wifstrand, A.   504 n. 19
Wiggermann, F. A. M.   682 n. 26
Williamson, H. G. M.   354 n. 24, 736 n. 15
Willi-Plein, I.   259 n. 4, 516 n. 9
Willis, J. T.   725 n. 1
Wills, L.   350 n. 11
Wilson, A. W.   350 n. 11
Wilson, E.   128 n. 4
Wilson, G. H.   410 n. 38
Wilson, S.   100 n. 14
Wise, M. O.   3 n. 5, 98 n. 10, 114 n. 5, 128 n. 5, 151 n. 2, 206 n. 5, 273 n. 16, 318 n. 41, 336 n. 1, 356 n. 31, 380 n. 3
Wolff, H. W.   263 n. 11
Woodsworth, J.   643 n. 15
Woodward, S. R.   72 n. 7
Woude, van der A. S.   76 n. 12, 323 n. 1, 332 n. 27, 467 n. 6
Wright, A.   409 n. 35
Wright, B.   606 n. 4
Wright, G. E.   152 n. 3, 228 n. 74, 325 n. 8, 439 n. 5
Würthwein, E.   845 n. 42

Yadin, Y.   29 n. 10, 72 n. 4, 120 nn. 23–24, 142 n. 52, 228 n. 76, 347 n. 3, 379 n. 1, 403 n. 14, 404 n. 18, 453 n. 1, 829 n. 10
Yalon, H.   338 n. 11
Yardeni, A.   117 n. 11
Yaron, R.   369 n. 12, 811 n. 3, 831 n. 21
Yule, G.   528 n. 12

Zakowitch, Y.   787 n. 61, 842 n. 28
Zalewski, S.   768 n. 16
Zangenberg, J.   143 n. 60
Zeitlin, S.   475 n. 35
Zenger, E.   242 n. 2, 246 n. 22, 249 n. 36
Zevit, Z.   205 n. 4, 368 n. 4
Zias, J.   72 n. 7, 143 n. 57
Ziegler, J.   243 nn. 6–7, 560 n. 4, 635 n. 4, 783 n. 50
Zimmerli, W.   621 n. 7
Zimmermann, J.   323 n. 3, 331 n. 24
Zipor, M. A.   790 n. 65
Zuckerman, B.   804 n. 31